Listen to Jesus Daily

A Collection of God's Revelations

LILY L. LOH

ISBN: 978-1-959312-00-0

Published by

PO Box 3619
Vista, CA 92084
www.eudistsusa.org

TABLE OF CONTENTS

DEDICATION

TO

my beloved

Jesus Christ

who suffered

and died

on the cross

for me

FOREWORD

by Rev. Msgr. Richard F. Duncanson
Retired Pastor

"Listen to God Daily," Lily Loh's previous book, was a delightful invitation to discover how God speaks to us as we read and reflect on the Scripture readings at Mass each day. Her new book, "Listen to Jesus Daily," renews her invitation to listen to God, but in an even more personal way, as she shares her visions and conversations with Jesus. Starting with a brief Scripture quote for each day of the year, Lily describes what she sees as she prayerfully meditates. She then tells us how Jesus speaks to her, explaining her vision and offering his words of comfort and encouragement. Each reflection then concludes with Lily's prayerful response to Jesus, reminding us that prayer is best understood as a personal conversation with Jesus. Hopefully, as we read this beautiful little book, we will learn how to meditate on the Scriptures, listen to Jesus speaking to us through them, and offer our own prayerful response to what Jesus has told us.

ACKNOWLEDGEMENTS

First of all I would like to thank all those who have encouraged me to journal and write down my meditations daily. Pauline Wright was the one who prayed over me many years ago and told me that she saw a pen standing over my head. She said that God was calling me to write. From that day on I started journaling after meditating on the readings for the daily Mass. Without Pauline's prophecy this book would never have come into being. I am forever grateful for all what she has done for me.

Special thanks to Dr. Bill Creasy who taught at UCLA and is an excellent teacher and storyteller. He made the Bible came alive for me with historical and geographical illustrations even though the events took place many years ago. I have studied the entire Bible from Genesis to Revelation with him over seven years. Since then I have grown spiritually closer to Jesus.

I want to thank Angie Lake who taught me how to read the Bible not just with my head but with my heart. She showed us in her class how to listen to God's words not only with our ears but with our soul. She emphasized that the Bible is a collection of love letters from God to each one of us and taught us how to write down our reflections and revelations from God to us through the scripture.

When I moved to Solana Beach, about forty years ago, I was very blessed to become a parishioner at St. James Church. Fr. John Howard has been a part of our family since I moved into that parish. He was the priest who married my daughter and baptized my four grandchildren. He also celebrated the funeral mass for my husband. Thanks to Fr. Howard, I got acquainted with the Eudist priests.

My gratitude to Steve Marshall who is in charge of the Eudist Press and has spent a lot of time and effort overseeing the production of this book and made it available to the public. Many thanks to all the people at the Eudist Press and the volunteers who worked so hard in designing, formatting and putting this book together for me.

I am forever grateful to my good friend, Marion Smith, who spend many hours proofreading my book for me. She told me that she enjoyed reading my book. It gave her a lot of pleasure while she was proofreading it. Thank you so much, Marion.

Many thanks to my family and friends who have kept me in their prayers, especially Helena Kim, Elise Botch, Maureen Mettee and many others at St. James Church. A special gratitude to my brothers and sisters, my family and my friends who enjoyed reading my first book, *Listen to God Daily*, so much that they inspired me and encouraged me to write another one like it.

I am most grateful to my God, our Father in heaven, for using me as His instrument to spread His eternal word to all those who are eager to hear them. Without Jesus this book would never be possible. Only with the help of the Holy Spirit who guided me and instructed me from the beginning to the end was I able to write my visions and revelations in this book. May God be glorified forever!

INTRODUCTION

After I finished writing my first spiritual book *Listen to God Daily*, I continued to meditate and journal every morning. A few years later I realized that I have enough material to write my second book on listening to Jesus who is the Son of our living God.

When I was baptized around twelve years old, I only knew God the Father. I could talk to Him like my own father. Shortly after I was baptized I became very ill with TB. It was during this time that I heard God speaking to me. I remember very clearly the day when I thought that I was going to die. I looked out my window with tears in my eyes telling God that I was too young to die and that I have not yet seen the world. I heard from the depth of my heart that God said, "Lily, you will see the world." From that moment on I became healthier and stronger every day. Since then I have travelled all around the world. God always keeps His promise.

My relationship with Jesus only started when I was at St. Mary's College during my first freshman year. I remember that day very well. It was during Lent when I was praying alone in front of a large wooden cross in the chapel. The more I contemplated the suffering of Jesus hanging on the cross the more I realized how much he really loved me. It was during this time when Jesus spoke straight to my heart that he loved me the moment I was conceived in my mother's womb. From that day on I grew closer and closer to him and even desired to be a nun so I could dedicate my life to serve him. But God had other plans for me. I got married instead and became a mother of two children, teacher, Eucharistic minister and prayer minister.

The reason I am writing this book is to encourage you to start meditating and listening to Jesus who loves us so much. His deepest desire is for us to love him more and more each day. Remember the story about Martha and Mary? Martha was not happy when her sister was sitting by Jesus' feet and not helping her in the kitchen. This is what Jesus answered her in reply, "Martha, Martha, you are anxious and worried about many things. There is need of only one thing. Mary has chosen the better part." (Luke 10:41-42)

When two people are in love it seems like they are always together talking and listening to each other. They want to spend every moment together. It is the same with Jesus. He longs to spend quality time alone with you. He wants you to know him better. So take time out of your busy schedule each day and sit quietly with him alone and have a heart to heart conversation with him. Jesus is thirsting for your love.

Here are a few tips to help you start listening to Jesus. Every morning I read the readings of the day for the Mass or from the Bible very slowly. Then I pick a sentence or a word that really speaks to me. I ask the Holy Spirit to open my heart and ears to hear Jesus better. Then I sit quietly for a few minutes and wait for him to speak to me. Since I am a very visual person, he often gives me a vision and then he explains to me what he wants me to learn from it. I always have my journal ready with a pen in my hand and start writing as soon as I hear him talking to me. This entire process usually takes only about fifteen minutes. In the beginning I only heard a few sentences from him and gradually he revealed himself to me more and more. You will be surprised that your relationship with Jesus will be transformed. I hope you will give it a try. Jesus loves you so much that he was willing to suffer and die on the cross for you.

May God bless you!
Lily L. Loh

JANUARY

BLESS YOU

> *"The Lord bless you and keep you! The Lord let his face shine upon you, and be gracious to you!"*
>
> NUMBERS 6:24-25

In my vision I saw Jesus praying alone in the garden. "My beloved, every time when you spend time with me I will bless you abundantly. You will be guided by the Holy Spirit and will be enlightened by my wisdom. Come away alone often to pray. It is through moments like this that you will be filled with my peace and joy. Prayer is a vital part of your spiritual growth. Every day block off a time when you can be alone with me. You will reap a hundred fold. Through prayer you will know what my Father's will is for you each day. I will lead you and guide you every step of the way."

> *O Jesus, my love and my redeemer. Thank you for all your blessings that you have bestowed upon me and my family.*

REFLECTION: Do I take time off each day to pray? Have I thanked Jesus for all his blessings upon me lately?

ANOINTING

"As for you, the anointing that you received
from him remains in you, so that you
do not need anyone to teach you."

1 JOHN 2:27

In my vision I saw myself sitting next to Jesus on the floor. There were many other people who were listening to him also. "My precious one, sit by me and I will teach you. Listen to my words and ponder them in your heart as my mother Mary did. You may not understand everything fully at first. But with the help of the Holy Spirit you will eventually understand and know the truth. Stay close to me and be ready to learn from me. I will change your heart and mind to the true meaning of life. You will be anointed with love, joy and peace."

Come, Lord Jesus, teach me and mold
me into your image and likeness. Anoint
me with your words of wisdom.

REFLECTION: How often do I sit quietly with Jesus alone and listen to his teaching?

LAMB OF GOD

*"The next day he saw Jesus coming toward
him and said, 'Behold, the Lamb of God,
who takes away the sin of the world."*

JOHN 1:29

In my vision I saw a woman kneeling and weeping at Jesus' feet. She was anointing him with fragrant oil and drying his feet with her hair. "My dear child, when you come to me for forgiveness of your sins, I will always wash you clean with my blood and water that came out from my side. I am the Lamb of God who has died and suffered on the cross for you. I have carried all your sins with me as I carried my cross to the Calvary. You are forgiven and washed clean. You have been set free from all your iniquities. Go in peace and sin no more."

*All loving and forgiving Jesus, thank you
for taking away all my sins on the cross.
Help me to avoid sin at all cost.*

REFLECTION: Do I truly believe that Jesus has forgiven me and washed me clean with his blood and water?

FOLLOWED JESUS

"The two disciples heard what he said and followed Jesus."

JOHN 1:37

In my vision I saw myself following Jesus on a narrow path. "My precious, when you follow me be ready to abandon the past. For I will take you places where you have never been. Do not be afraid to leave your familiar environment, but ready to depart and follow me wherever I will lead you. To be my disciple is to surrender yourself totally so that you can be useful in building my kingdom. My kingdom is not of this world. When you follow me, you need to abandon your own agenda -- because you cannot be in two places at the same time. Either you are with me or you are not. That is your choice."

Yes, Lord Jesus, I will follow you wherever you are leading me. Jesus, I trust in you and I have faith in you.

REFLECTION: Am I willing to follow Jesus and be his disciple?

DEED

> *"Children, let us not love in word or*
> *speech but in deed and truth."*
>
> 1 JOHN 3:18

In my vision I saw Jesus carrying the heavy cross. He was suffering in pain with each step. "My beloved, there is no greater love than the one who lays down his life for another. Whatever you do to the least of my brothers you do it to me. When you see a person in need of help or healing, go and minister to him as you would do for me. I love everyone in this world because I created them in my image and likeness. Whenever you go out of your way to help others for the glory of God you will be rewarded greatly. Be my hands and feet for them. Be my compassionate and loving heart to them."

> *Compassionate and loving Jesus, change my*
> *heart to be more like yours, so that I will*
> *be able to love others as you love me.*

REFLECTION: Do I go out of my way to help others in need?

THE STAR

"They were overjoyed at seeing the star,
and on entering the house they saw
the child with Mary his mother."

MATTHEW 2: 10-11

In my vision I saw the three wise men who were following the star that lead them to baby Jesus. "My child, search me and you will find me. Everyone who desires to come close to me will be led by the Holy Spirit. He will guide you to me and give you the knowledge and the wisdom. Never stop searching. Seek and you shall find. Like the three wise men you too will be overjoyed when you finally find me. Your life will be transformed and changed. You will have an inner joy. This joy is knowing that you are a child of God and I came to save you."

Most loving Jesus, I love you and I adore
you. My heart is restless until it rests in you
who are all good and deserve all my love.

REFLECTION: When was the last time I actually tried to seek Jesus in my daily life circumstances?

LIFE

> *"Whoever possesses the Son has life; whoever does*
> *not possess the Son of God does not have life."*
>
> 1 JOHN 5:12

In my vision I saw myself drawing water by the river with Jesus helping me by my side. "My precious one, when you have me you will have life. For with me you will lack nothing. You will have abundant life. Life is like a river that flows and never stops. You have only one life to live. Live each day with me by my side. You will have endless living water that you need to nourish and to replenish your weary soul. Live each day with joy, for there is nothing you will lack. I am all you need. Sing praise and give thanks for your life. It is the most important and precious gift I have given you."

> *I thank you and praise you, Jesus, for*
> *giving me life here on earth and life*
> *after death with you in heaven.*

REFLECTION: Do I realize that Jesus is all I need and without him I have no life?

DO NOT BE AFRAID

*"'Take courage, it is I, do not be afraid.' He got
into the boat with them and the wind died down."*

MARK 6:50-51

In my vision I saw myself in a small rowing boat. It was tossing left and right. But the minute Jesus got into my boat everything became calm. "My love, invite me into your heart and I will calm your nerves. You will have nothing to fear when you know that I am with you. Fear only comes when you think you have to face your problems alone. Fear cripples you. Be assured that I am with you always. Anywhere you are there I will be. Any time you call on me I will help you. You are never alone. You can be sure on that. Trust in me with your whole heart. Peace be with you."

*Jesus, my Lord and my God, you are my
savior and my redeemer. In you I place
my trust. Fill me with your peace.*

REFLECTION: When I am afraid do I know that Jesus is always by my side and ready to help me?

GLORIFY THE LORD

"Glorify the Lord, Jerusalem; Zion,
offer praise to your God, for he has
strengthened the bars of your gates."
PSALM 147:12-13

In my vision I saw a man with his hands raised dancing and praising God. "My loving child, every time when you praise me you are glorifying me. It is the highest form of prayer. When you pray, pray from your heart. Pray with your hands raised and eyes focused on me. Your prayers will be like a sweet incense rising into heaven. It gladdens me to hear you pray when your heart is full of gratitude instead of reciting one petition after another. Sing praise and dance before me like a child full of joy and give thanks for all that I have done for you."

I thank you and praise you, Lord Jesus. You
are worthy and precious to me. I love you
and glorify you forever and ever. Amen.

REFLECTION: How often do I give thanks and praise to Jesus so that he may be glorified?

TESTIMONY

> *"And this is the testimony: God gave us*
> *eternal life, and this life is in his Son."*
>
> 1 JOHN 5:11

In my vision I was in a courtroom on the stand and when I looked up I saw Jesus standing there. I knew instantly that I will be set free with him being my lawyer. "My beloved child, yes, when you believe in me, you have nothing to fear. You know that I will set you free and you will live with me for eternity in heaven. Isn't it comforting to know? And yet, many people do not accept me and rather live a life that will lead them to death. My precious one, when you have me, you have everything. There is nothing I will not do for you. All you need to do is to believe in me and trust in me."

> *My Jesus, I do believe in your saving*
> *power. I know with you I will have eternal*
> *life. Without you I will surely perish.*

REFLECTION: Do I believe that I will be saved because of the saving power of Jesus?

CONFIDENCE IN HIM

*"And we have confidence in him, that if we ask
anything according to his will, he hears us."*

1 JOHN 5:14

In my vision I saw a woman trying to touch Jesus' garment. She had confidence that if she just touched the hem of his cloak she would be healed. "My child, have that kind of confidence and faith in me. You know that I want you to be healed. For I came into this world to set you free from all your sicknesses and sin. By my wounds you are healed. Have faith in me. Know that I am God and nothing is impossible for me. It saddens me when people do not realize that I am the healer. I can caste out evil spirits and demons. Nothing is too difficult for me. Ask and you shall receive."

*Lord Jesus, you are my healer and my
savior. Everything is possible with you.
Heal me O Lord and I will be healed.*

REFLECTION: When I am sick, do I ask Jesus to heal me? If not, why not?

PARTNERS OF CHRIST

*"We have become partners of Christ
if only we only hold the beginning of
the reality firm until the end."*

Hebrews 3:14

In my vision I saw myself yoked together with Jesus working in a field. "My beloved, to be my partner you need to be yoked with me. This way we work together in unison and towards the same goal. Never go ahead of me nor stay behind me, but walk with me side by side. Let me guide you and direct you each step of the way. Only in this way there will be a great harvest. Be obedient to my promptings and go with me until the end. Without perseverance you will never be able to bear much fruit. Stay focused and stay alert. Your reward will be great in heaven."

*Dear Jesus, I know your yoke is easy and
burden light. Help me to do your will until the
day when I will be united with you forever.*

REFLECTION: Am I yoked with Jesus in every task I do each day?

COME AFTER ME

> *"Whoever wishes to come after me must deny himself, take up his cross, and follow me."*
>
> MARK 8:34

In my vision I saw two paths. One was full of street lights and signs of shows and diners. The other path where Jesus was walking was a barren and narrow road. "My dear child, you have a choice to follow me or to follow the earthly pleasures. When you come after me be prepared to give up all your own cravings and be ready to give your life to me according to my will. For my will for you is eternal life. So do not be afraid to take up your cross and follow me. I will lead you to the right path. I will lead you to my Father who loves you with an everlasting love."

> *Thank you, Jesus, for showing me the way. I will carry my cross and go after you to my Father's house.*

REFLECTION: Do I find it difficult to carry my cross and follow Jesus daily?

HEAR HIS VOICE

*"Oh, that today you would hear his voice: do
not harden your hearts as at Meribah."*

Psalm 95: 7-8

In my vision I saw Jesus teaching a crowd at a mountain side. "My beloved, when you spend quiet time alone with me you will hear my voice. I am your good shepherd. I take care of all your needs. If you are following my teaching I will tell you where to go and what to do. You are never alone. So talk to me often and listen to my voice. I will be your teacher and your good shepherd. If you follow my instructions you will never get lost but will reap abundant blessings. For I only want the best for you. So be still and hear my voice each day and I will guide you on the road to true happiness."

*Lord Jesus, my good shepherd, I want
to hear your voice always and follow
you wherever you are leading me.*

REFLECTION: Do I take time out every day to listen to Jesus and follow his instructions?

OBEDIENCE

> *"Obedience is better than sacrifice, to*
> *listen, better than the fat of rams."*
>
> 1 SAMUEL 15:22

In my vision I saw Jesus kneeling and praying fervently in the garden of Gethsemane. "My loving child, it is not easy to follow the will of my Father. The cup that I had to drink was so painful just thinking about it made my sweat became like drops of blood. But I was obedient to my Father unto death. That is how you are redeemed. Through my obedience you are set free. Adam and Eve disobeyed my Father by eating the forbidden fruit. I came to die on the cross in obedience to my Father so that you will have eternal life. Be an imitator of me. Obey every commandment and follow all the laws and you will be saved. A new commandment I give to you is to love one another as I love you."

> *Yes, Lord Jesus, I will obey everything you*
> *have taught me. I will love my neighbor as you*
> *love me. Thank you, Jesus, for saving me.*

REFLECTION: Am I obedient to the commandments and do I follow the laws?

FAST

> *"The disciples of John and of the*
> *Pharisees were accustomed to fast."*
> MARK 2:18

In my vision I saw Jesus breaking bread and giving it to his disciples to eat. "My child, fasting is good for your soul. When you fast you are more atoned with those who are less fortunate than yourself especially those people who have no food or shelter. Fasting will make you more compassionate and loving. You will understand more what others are going through especially those who are poor and helpless. Many people in this world go to bed hungry. Share what you have with all those who ask from you. Share not only food but also your time and talent with them. You will be rewarded a hundred fold."

> *Compassionate Jesus, you are the most loving*
> *and caring person in the world. I want to imitate*
> *you in all you do. Enlarge my heart, Lord.*

REFLECTION: How often do I fast for all that Jesus has suffered for me on the cross?

FORGIVE SINS

"That you may know that the Son of Man
has authority to forgive sins on earth."

MARK 2:10

In my vision I saw a teacher erasing all the words that a child had written on a blackboard. "My precious one, I am in charge of the entire universe. I have the authority to forgive sins and to set you free. When you sin you are going the wrong way. I can easily bring you back to the right path. But I will never force you to do anything that you do not want to do. I gave you a free will. First you must want to change your ways and acknowledge your wrongdoing. When you are ready to confess and repent for your sins I will be waiting for you to welcome you back with my open arms."

Lord, I am heartily sorry for all my sins.
Thank you for forgiving me and setting
me free from all my guilt and shame.

REFLECTION: Do I believe that Jesus has authority to forgive sins no matter how seriously I have sinned?

PRIEST

"You are a priest forever in the manner of Melchizedek."

PSALM 110:4

In my vision I saw Jesus all dressed in his priestly robe offering sacrifice for us at the altar. "My child, I am the high priest sent to atone for your sins. I came to sacrifice myself for you so that you will have eternal life with me in heaven. I have redeemed you with my blood and have called you by name. When you were baptized, you too were called to be a priest to intercede for others and to bring them to my Father. A priest's duty is to offer sacrifice with prayers and petitions for others. Do likewise and you and your family will be saved."

Lord Jesus, you are a priest forever in the order of Melchizedek. May you be praised and glorified forever.

REFLECTION: Do I pray and intercede for others especially when they need God's help?

INTERCESSION

"Jesus is always able to save those who approach God through him, since he lives forever to make intercession for them."

HEBREW 7:25

In my vision I saw Jesus kneeling amongst olive trees and praying fervently to his heavenly Father. "My loving child, I am always praying for you and your family. For I love each of you more than you can ever imagine. You are my precious creations and I only want the best for you. Trust in my prayers. Trust in me. For I intercede for you and all your loved ones. If you only knew the power of prayer, you would pray constantly without ceasing. Every prayer is heard in heaven. Every petition is answered. You need not fear that you are alone when you pray. I am praying with you and for you."

My loving Jesus, thank you for interceding for me and my family. Jesus, I trust in you with all my heart.

REFLECTION: Am I aware that Jesus is always praying for me and my loved ones?

SNATCHED ME

*"For you have snatched me from death, kept
my feet from stumbling, that I may walk
before God in the light of the living."*

PSALM 56:14

In my vision I saw myself walking on a bed of rocks trying to reach to the top of the mountain. "My child, alone you cannot make it. But with me by your side helping you eventually you will reach your destination. Therefore never go anywhere without my assistance. This way you will not be lost. Hold my hand and I will lead you to eternal life. Without me you can do nothing. With me everything is possible. Lean on me when the path becomes too strenuous. I will carry you and uphold you. Trust in me and keep your eyes on me. Only in this way you will walk in my light."

*O Lord, rescue me from all my perils.
Be with me when I am in trouble. For
you are my rock and my salvation.*

REFLECTION: When I am in trouble do I remember to call on Jesus to help me?

MERCY

*"Have mercy on me, God, have mercy
on me. In you I seek refuge."*

Psalm 57:2

In my vision I saw myself kneeling and bowing down in front of Jesus and asking for his forgiveness and mercy. "My precious child, everyone who comes to me for mercy will receive it back tenfold. For I am a merciful God, slow to anger and full of compassion. Every time you ask for my forgiveness I will always forgive you. I will wash away your guilt and shame with my precious blood. Your sins I will remember no more after you have repented and confessed. Your heart will be as clean as snow. You are set free. Like an eagle you will soar again. For I love a humble heart. Be merciful to others as I have been to you. Peace be with you."

*Merciful Jesus, you are so loving and
forgiving. Thank you for washing me
clean and restoring me to life.*

REFLECTION: Am I merciful to others as Jesus has been with me?

FISHERS OF MEN

"Jesus said to them, 'Come after me, and
I will make you fishers of men.'"

MARK 1:17

In my vision I saw Jesus calling Peter and Andrew to follow him while they were cleaning their nets. "My dear child, I am calling you also to leave your own plans aside. Are you willing to follow me? I will be able to use you wherever there is a need. People are suffering and need your love and prayers. I have called you to minister to all who need healing, not only physically but emotionally and spiritually too. They need to hear the good news about me. I have no more hands and feet to work in this world. Will you be my hands and feet? There is so much to be done. The harvest is ready but the laborers are few. Go forth and bring hope and joy to all those in need of my love.

Thank you, Jesus, for calling me. Yes, I
will be your hands and feet to all those
who are in need of your healing love.

REFLECTION: Am I willing to be a fisher of men for Jesus?

APOSTLES

"He appointed twelve, whom he also named apostles, that they might be with him and he might send them forth to preach and to have authority to drive out demons."

MARK 3:14-15

In my vision I saw a group of mailmen all ready to go out and deliver mail to people. "My child, you are also called to go out and bring the good news to others like my apostles. You are equipped to speak in my name. I will fill you with the Holy Spirit and he will guide you on your way. You do not go out alone. Your guardian angel will go with you. He will protect you from all harm. You will be given the right words to speak when you are my witness. You will have power over the evil one. In my name you will be able to heal others and drive out demons. Do not be afraid nor worried when you are on a mission. I will always go with you and guide you. Go in peace."

Lord Jesus, thank you for choosing me to be your disciple. I want to serve you always.

REFLECTION: Do I realize that Jesus has given me power to overcome evil and to heal others in his name?

RICH SOIL

> *"Those sown on rich soil are the ones who hear the word and accept it and bear fruit thirty and sixty and a hundred fold."*
>
> MARK 4:20

In my vision I saw a cornfield ready to be harvested. "My beloved, everyone who hears my word and follows me will bear much fruit. First you must have a heart ready to receive the Holy Spirit. Then you need to follow through by going out and doing it. Study my word day and night. My word is like living water which makes all things grow. Without my water the soil will be dry and unable to produce much fruit. Spend time cultivating the soil so that it will be able to absorb all the water when it rains. Prayer is necessary in making anything to happen. Without prayer there will be no fruit. It is through prayer you will be able to bear fruit, thirty and a hundred fold. Pray, study my word and go out and do all that I have planned for you to do."

Loving Jesus, your word is my living water. Without you I can do nothing.

REFLECTION: Do I believe that when I study the word of God I will be able to produce much fruit?

BAPTIZED

"Whoever believes and is baptized will be saved;
whoever does not believe will be condemned."

MARK 16: 16

In my vision I saw John the Baptist pouring water over Jesus in the river Jordan. "My child, anyone who is baptized becomes a child of God and he will be saved. Those who are not baptized nor believes in me will not enter into heaven. You, my precious one, are chosen to share this good news with others. You will bring souls to me, especially those who still do not know me nor love me. They need to hear that I came into the world to save them and not to condemn them. My deepest desire is that all unbelievers will be converted and baptized so that they can also enjoy the eternity with me in heaven. For I came and died on the cross for everyone."

Loving Jesus, I do believe that you are
the Son of almighty God. Give me the
courage to go out and proclaim the good
news to those who are not yet baptized.

REFLECTION: Have I told others that they may be saved through baptism because of Jesus?

LAY HANDS

> *"They will lay hands on the sick,*
> *and they will recover."*
> MARK 16:18

In my vision I saw a pair of hands radiant with light. "My faithful servant, I have no hands in the world now. If you let me use your hands to heal people, your hands will be radiant with my healing light. Whoever you touch when you pray in my name, they will be healed. My healing power will be upon you whenever you call upon my name. You will speak words of comfort and encouragement to them and they will be healed. For nothing is impossible with me. Trust in my healing power. Call on me and whatever you ask in my name I will do it. Go and lay hands on the sick and I will heal them."

> *O Lord Jesus, you are the healer and*
> *the redeemer. Use me and my hands to*
> *heal the sick. I am your servant.*

REFLECTION: Have I been hesitant to lay hands on the sick and pray with them in the name of Jesus for healing?

DO NOT WORRY

"Do not worry about tomorrow;
tomorrow will take care of itself.
Sufficient for a day is its own evil."

MATTHEW 6:34

In my vision I saw a poor woman put a coin into the temple treasury. "My child, that widow trusted me with all her heart. She gave away the only coin she had because she believed that I would provide for her all her needs. She was not worried about her future because she knew that I cared about her and loved her. She had full confidence in me knowing that I would never forsake her. There is always hope. She would never starve to death. She knew that I am a loving and caring God who would provide for her. The more you trust me, the more miracles you will see. So do not worry about tomorrow. I will always take good care of you too."

Precious Jesus, thank you for your
words of comfort and reassurance.
Jesus, I place my trust in you.

REFLECTION: Do I worry about what will happen tomorrow or in the future? Do I really trust in Jesus?

NOTHING IS SECRET

*"For there is nothing hidden except
to be made visible; nothing is secret
except to come to the light."*

MARK 4:22

In my vision I saw myself walk into a brightly lit room.
"My precious one, I am the light of the world. Nothing
is hidden away from me. I know every hair on your head
and every deed that you do in the dark. No secret can be
hidden from my all-knowing knowledge. Be not afraid.
I did not come into the world to condemn you but to
redeem you. I will forgive every sin that you have committed in the darkness and in the secrecy of your heart.
Come to me and repent of your sins and you will be
made clean. You will be set free and become a new creation again."

*My loving and forgiving Jesus, thank you
for your mercy and compassion for me.
Thank you for your redeeming love.*

REFLECTION: Am I afraid to bare my soul to Jesus
even though he already knows everything about me?

MY SHIELD

"But you, Lord, are a shield around me,
my glory, you keep my head high."

PSALM 3:4

In my vision I saw myself in an astronaut suit. "My child, you are protected from all harm when you put on my armor. It will ward off all enemies. No arrow can penetrate you to harm you. You can breathe easily knowing that I am with you. Every step you take you are guarded so that you will not fall nor stumble. You will walk with your head held high knowing that I am with you. You are enveloped with my love and protection. You are watched and monitored every step of the way. I know when you sit or stand. I know every move you make. You are never alone. For you are precious to me and I only want what is best for you. Go forth and know that I am your shield and your strength."

Most caring Jesus, you are my rock and my
shield. With you I have nothing to fear.

REFLECTION: Is Jesus my shield and my protector in every situation of my life?

BROTHERS AND SISTERS

"Whoever does the will of God is my brother and sister and mother."

MARK 3:35

In my vision I saw Jesus sitting in a living room teaching to a large group of people. His mother and brothers were standing outside the house trying to get in. "My beloved, you are my brother and sister because you listen to me and are always ready to do my will. When the Angel Gabriel appeared to my mother Mary, her answer was, 'Be it done according to your will.' She sacrificed her own will and did everything according to what my Father wants her to do. She stood by me at the foot of the cross and was with me when I took my last breath. She is a model for you to follow."

Loving Jesus, to do your will is my delight. I want to live each day for your honor and glory, Lord.

REFLECTION: Am I willing to put aside my own plans and do the will of God, as Jesus called me to do?

ENDURANCE

*"You need endurance to do the will of God
and receive what he has promised."*

HEBREWS 10:36

In my vision I saw Jesus so weak and tired from carrying his cross that he fell three times. "My faithful one, see how I endured till the end? I accomplished what I was born to do by dying on the cross for the sins of the world. I paid for your redemption. You are set free only because I endured till the end. So do not despair nor give up. Keep one foot in front of another. I am with you and will support you. When your cross is too heavy, I will carry it with you. I will send people to help you along your way and my mother to comfort you. Do not be afraid. Take courage and you too will reach heaven one day."

*Here I am Lord. I come to do your
will. I have full confidence in you, Jesus,
that you will help me till the end.*

REFLECTION: When my cross becomes so heavy do I remember to ask Jesus to help me and to carry it with me?

FEBRUARY

YOUR LIGHT

> *"Your light must shine before others,*
> *that they may see your good deeds and*
> *glorify your heavenly Father."*
> MATHEW 5:16

In my vision I was standing face to face in front of Jesus. His face was aglow with radiant light. The more time I spent in front of him, the brighter my face became. "Yes, my child, I am the light of the world. When you spend time with me, your face will become aglow with my light. When you go out to minister to others, they will see the light on your face and will glorify God for all that I have done for you. Like Moses, bring the light into this darkened world. You are my light. Go forth and let your light shine upon all those who need my light."

> *Lord Jesus, you are the light of the world. Let*
> *your light shine upon me and on others. Enlighten*
> *our minds and purify our souls with your light.*

REFLECTION: How often do I help others in need so that they can see the light of Christ in me?

KING OF GLORY

"Lift up your heads, O gates; rise up, you ancient portals, that the king of glory may enter."

PSALM 24:9

In my vision I saw Jesus standing outside a door knocking. "My child, I am knocking at your heart. Will you open and receive me? Will you welcome me into every aspect of your life? I long to come and dwell in your heart. I want to be a part of your daily life. Will you invite me in? I want to dine with you and go places with you. Talk to me and share your joys and sorrows with me. For you are my precious child and I miss you when you are far away from me. Will you be my friend? When you do, I will bless you and your family abundantly. When you glorify me I will shower you with my graces.

Yes, my loving Jesus, please come into my heart. I want to be your best friend so that I can praise you and glorify you forever.

REFLECTION: Am I ready to invite Jesus into my heart and have dinner with him?

PREACHING

"So he went into their synagogues,
preaching and driving out demons
throughout the whole of Galilee."

MARK 1:39

In my vision I saw Jesus sitting in front of the Jewish people teaching them about the truth in the temple. "My beloved, people need to hear the word of God. Without my word they will perish. For my word has life and power. Whoever listens to my word and follows it will live an abundant life. A life full of joy and hope. Those who do not will have to struggle through every day without my guidance. Sit by me and learn from my teaching. Your life will be transformed. Follow my word and you shall live. Now go and preach to others so they too will have an abundant life."

Thank you, Lord Jesus, for your preaching
and teaching. Your word is a lamp to my feet
and will guide me throughout the day.

REFLECTION: Do I have the courage to go and tell others about Jesus and his teachings?

HE CURED MANY

"He cured many who were sick with various diseases, and he drove out many demons, not permitting them to speak because they knew him."

MARK 1:34

In my vision I saw Jesus laying his hands on the sick. Everyone who came to him was healed. They were filled with joy and praising God. "My child, I came into this world to heal and to save. I want people to know that my Father and I love you so much that I am willing to suffer and die on the cross for your sins. Everyone who believes in me and asks for healing will be healed. Have faith in my healing power. Do not be afraid to come and touch me. Remember how I healed the 10 lepers. Unfortunately only one came back to thank me. Be grateful for everything you have received."

Gracious Jesus, you are my healer and my redeemer. Thank you for healing all my illnesses and diseases.

REFLECTIONS: Do I believe that Jesus has the power to heal the sick? Have I been healed by him?

SUPREME GOOD

"I even consider everything as a loss because of the
supreme good of knowing Christ Jesus my Lord."

PHILIPPIANS 3:8

In my vision I saw a very large and brilliant diamond. "My love, I am worth more than the large diamond you saw in your vision. Treasure me above everything else. Not everyone realizes how blessed they are when they have me. You know that when you have me in your heart you have everything. With me you have salvation, redemption and forgiveness. With me you will spend eternity in heaven. Seek me first and your life will never be the same again. Show everyone your treasure like a young girl showing off her diamond ring to her friends. I am your supreme good."

You, O Lord, are more precious than
diamonds or gold to me. You are my
treasure and my beloved spouse.

REFLECTION: Do I treasure Jesus above anything else even more than diamond or gold?

PEACE WITH EVERYONE

*"Strive for peace with everyone, and for that
holiness without which no one will see the Lord."*

HEBREWS 12:14

In my vision I saw Jesus standing in front of his disciples
in his resurrected body. He said to them, "Peace be with
you." "My loving child, when you are with me you will
have peace and you will be at peace with others. With
me all your actions will be transformed and pleasing to
God my Father. So start each day by inviting me into
your heart. Let me reign in you and you will have peace
all day long with yourself and with others. Let my love
shine to all you meet each day. Love can change hearts
and has power to heal all hurts. Go in peace."

*Lord Jesus, you are the Prince of Peace.
Fill me with your love and peace so
that I will be holy in your sight.*

REFLECTION: Do I strive for peace with everyone
even those who do not like me?

THEY LEFT EVERYTHING

"When they brought their boats to the shore,
they left everything and followed him."

LUKE 5:11

In my vision I saw a funeral and people were going to say their last farewell to the deceased before the body is taken away to be buried. "My child, you came into this world with nothing and when you die you will not bring anything with you to heaven. Remember that everything you have now has no value at the end. Do not grow attached to things. The only thing that is of value is love and relationships with me and with others. Put love of people above all earthly possessions. Only then you can be my disciple. Come and follow me."

Lord, you are my most precious possession.
Fill me with more of your love so that
I can love others as you love me.

REFLECTION: Am I ready to leave everything and follow Jesus anywhere he wants me to go?

DEFILE

"Nothing that enters one from outside can defile that person; but the things that come out from within are what defile."

MARK 7:15

In my vision I saw a pure white heart full of radiant light. "My beloved, it is what comes out of your heart that counts. Anyone who has selfish and evil thoughts can defile not only himself but others. Anyone who is loving, kind and compassionate has a pure heart and will be pleasing to God and to others. It is the heart that defiles. So keep your heart clean and pure. Go to confession often and do nothing evil to tarnish your pure heart. Think before you speak, pray before you act and at all times do everything for the honor and glory of God."

Loving Jesus, purify my heart so that everything I do and say will be pleasing to you.

REFLECTION: How often do I go to confession to keep my heart clean and pure in God's eyes?

DO GOOD

"Do not neglect to do good and to share what you have; God is pleased by sacrifices of that kind."

Hebrews 13:16

In my vision I saw Jesus washing his disciples' feet at the last supper. "My precious one, do you see how I knelt down to wash my disciples' feet and served them like a slave? You too must do good to others as I have done for you. It takes sacrifice and hard work to serve others. But your reward will be great in heaven. It is through your humble service that others will learn the true meaning of love. There is no greater love than one who lays down his life for another. Imitate me in all you do. Through service you will find joy and peace. Do not let one day go by without doing at least one good deed."

My Jesus, fill me with more of your love so that I will be able to go out and do good for others. Give me a generous heart!

REFLECTION: Am I willing to wash other people's feet like Jesus did?

STRENGTHENED MY SPIRIT

*"On the day I cried out, you answered;
you strengthened my spirit."*

PSALM 138:3

In my vision I saw Samson; even though he was blind, when he prayed he was able to topple the pillars and killed the Philippians. "My child, with me you too will have the strength to destroy all the evil spirits that surround you every day. Make sure to call on me before you go out to proclaim the good news. The evil one is always ready to prevent you from doing good. Put on the armor of God daily. Pray and ask your guardian angel to protect you from all harm. You will have the authority and the strength to carry out all that I have planned for you to do. So have no fear but be strengthened with my spirit."

*Thank you, Lord Jesus, for always answering
my prayers. You are my rock and my strength.*

REFLECTION: Do I have the confidence that Jesus will give me the strength to accomplish all that needs to be done?

GLORY OF GOD

"Whether you eat or drink, or whatever you do, do everything for the glory of God."

1 CORINTHIANS 10:31

In my vision I saw Paul kneeling in front of the throne of God with his hands raised praising and glorifying God. "My faithful one, do everything for the glory of God. See how faithful Paul was? He dedicated his life doing my will since the day he saw me on the road to Damascus. He always asked me where I wanted to send him and what I wanted him to do. He was my faithful servant. He persevered until the end. He lived each day for me and for my glory. He suffered tremendously. All his sacrifice and effort produced much fruit. You too are called to proclaim the good news to others. Only in this way I will be glorified and praised forever."

Lord, I will do anything for you. May you be glorified and praised forever.

REFLECTION: Do I remember to do everything for the glory of God?

TRIALS

> *"Consider it all joy, my brothers, when you encounter various trials, for you know that the testing of your faith produces perseverance."*
>
> JAMES 1:2-3

In my vision I saw Jesus carrying a heavy cross and falling down three times until he reached Golgotha. "My beloved, do not give up when you are under trials. Lean on me and know that I am helping you. I will send angels to be with you and to guide you on your journey. Do not give up. Because trials will strengthen your faith in me. Trials will bring you closer to me and make you more humble. Pray often and know that I am always with you. You will never go through trials alone. With me at your side you will reach sainthood. You will develop character and endurance. Have total faith in me."

My loving Jesus, I do trust in you. Help me to always call on you when I am going through trials.

REFLECTION: Am I joyful, even during trials, knowing that everything works for good for those who love Jesus?

EVIL THOUGHTS

"From within people, from their hearts,
come evil thoughts, unchastity, theft, murder,
adultery, greed, malice, deceit, licentiousness,
envy, blasphemy, arrogance, folly."

MARK 7:21-22

In my vision I saw Judas receiving money from a Pharisee and promising to lead the solders to capture Jesus. "My child, have no evil thoughts in your heart but fill it with praise and thanksgiving. Do not be greedy nor envious of others. These are all sinful thoughts that will lead you to be defiled. All sinful acts and thoughts come from the evil one. He comes to destroy and to tempt you. Focus your thoughts on higher good. Love everything that is from God. Follow my commandments day after day. Study my words and memorize them. Fill your mind with positive things and love unceasingly."

Lord Jesus, you are all wise and
knowledgeable. I want to be holy and pure.
Help me to caste away all evil thoughts.

REFLECTION: How often do I focus my thoughts on Jesus instead of the evil and sinful things?

LISTEN TO HIM

"This is my beloved Son. Listen to him."

MARK 9:7

In my vision I saw Jesus teaching his disciples who were sitting all around him with great attention. "My children, if you want to be my disciple you must learn to listen to me. Because a disciple only does what the teacher tells him to do. How can you know my Father's will? Only through listening to me. Because I only do what my Father tells me to do. I never go out and do my own will. To be a good disciple you must be able to hear my voice and know my commandments. I will guide you and prompt you on the right path. Spend quiet time alone with me often and you will hear my voice."

Open my ears and my heart to hear you and to listen to your voice daily. I want to be your disciple, my Lord and my God.

REFLECTION: Do I take time off to listen to Jesus every day and follow him instead of my own agenda?

DENY HIMSELF

"If anyone wishes to come after me, he must deny himself and take up his cross daily and follow me."

LUKE 9:23

In my vision I saw John and Andrew following Jesus. "My child, when you come to follow me it means that you have to give up your own agenda and change your course of direction and go where I want to go. Many people are afraid to venture into the unknown. Not everyone can be my disciple -- only those who are willing to take a risk to follow me. John and Andrew spent an afternoon with me. They were so inspired that they went to bring their brothers with them to follow me also. I can use you too if you are willing to deny yourself and take up your cross daily."

My loving Jesus, help me to always be ready to obey you and to follow you wherever you are leading me.

REFLECTION: Am I ready to deny myself and carry my cross like Jesus?

IF YOU FORGIVE

"If you forgive others their transgressions,
your heavenly Father will forgive you."

MATTHEW 6:14

In my vision I saw Peter running away in total remorse after denying Jesus three times. "My beloved, when you have been forgiven for your sins, you will be transformed. Like Peter, you will know how much I really love you when you experience the power of being forgiven. Your heart will be softened with my love. As a result of this, you will be able to love and forgive others as I have done for you. It is a day of rejoicing when you know that you have been forgiven. Be not afraid to confess your sins. It will liberate you and set you free. Go and forgive others as I have forgiven you."

Lord Jesus, please forgive me for all
my past sins. Thank you for setting me
free from my guilt and shame.

REFLECTION: Have I forgiven everyone who has hurt me in the past?

ASHAMED OF ME

> *"Whoever is ashamed of me and of my words
> in this faithless and sinful generation, the Son
> of Man will be ashamed of when he comes
> in his Father's glory with the holy angels."*
>
> MARK 8:38

In my vision I saw myself standing in front of a bright shining sun. All around me there were black clouds, thunder and lightning. "My child, always seek me first and turn your back against this faithless and evil world. For when you acknowledge me to the world, I will acknowledge you to my Father. Every time when you follow my commandments you will be glorifying Him. But every time when you deny me, you will be denied by my Father also. For my Father and I are one. Whatever you do in my name, he will be glorified and honored."

> *Yes, my precious Jesus, I will go and tell others
> about you. For I love you and I want to give
> all the glory to you and to your Father.*

REFLECTION: How many times have I denied and been ashamed to talk about Jesus in front of others?

CROWN OF LIFE

*"Blessed is the man who perseveres in
temptation, for when he has been proved
he will receive the crown of life that he
promised to those who love him."*

JAMES 1:12

In my vision I saw two children standing in front of two
paths. One had candies on each side of the road and
the other had flowers that lead to an open beach with
blue ocean. "My little one, avoid temptation at all cost.
It always seems so sweet and fulfills your desires when
you are tempted by the evil one. Do not go down that
path that leads you to destruction and death. Choose
life. Choose to follow my footsteps. Pick up your cross
and come after me. For I will lead you to eternal salvation. When you are following my way you will receive
the crown of life."

*Help me, O Lord, to avoid all temptations.
I want to follow you always.*

REFLECTION: Do I try my best to overcome temptations so that I will receive the crown of life one day?

SLOW TO ANGER

"Everyone should be quick to listen, slow to speak, slow to anger, for anger does not accomplish the righteousness of God."

JAMES 1:19-20

This morning God gave me two visions: 1. a little child was throwing toys and breaking them because he was angry with his brother. 2. I was sitting on an inner tube flowing down a river. "My child, you can choose to get angry and destroy everything around you or you can surrender to my will. Feeling angry is not a sin, but what you do when you are angry can destroy people and things which you will regret later. Be slow to anger. Bring the issue to me. Talk it over with me. Never act in haste. Think before you act. Ask me to help you. Only then will you regain your peace and joy."

My Jesus, help me to hold my tongue and be slow to anger. I choose to forgive those who have hurt me.

REFLECTION: Do I ask Jesus for his advice when I am angry with someone or dealing with a difficult issue?

LOVE YOUR ENEMIES

> *"Love your enemies, and pray for those*
> *who persecute you, that you may be*
> *children of your heavenly Father."*
>
> MATHEW 5:44-45

In my vision I saw two men fighting with their swords with hatred in their eyes. "My loving child, never return evil with evil. Only love can change any relationship. With love you can change your enemies' hearts. With sword you will die by the sword. Those who have hatred in their hearts have no room for mercy and compassion. They will perish and suffer with their own wrongdoings. Those who love will reap goodness and kindness everywhere they go. Choose mercy and forgiveness and you will be filled with my love and become a child of my heavenly Father."

> *Loving Jesus, fill my heart with more of your*
> *love so that I will be able to love everyone*
> *-- even those who are my enemies.*

REFLECTION: Do I try to avoid being near my enemies and having hatred in my heart for them?

FORTY DAYS

> *"'Forty days more and Nineveh shall
> be overthrown,' the people of Nineveh
> believed God; they proclaimed a fast."*
>
> JONAH 3:4-5

In my vision I saw Jesus fasting and praying in the desert for 40 days. "My beloved, it is good to fast and repent your sins. This is the only way you will be able to conquer the evil one. The more you sacrifice yourself for God's sake, the more effective your prayer will be. When you fast, the evil one will flee -- because he knows that you are serious about doing God's will. That is why I went to the desert for 40 days before I started to proclaim the kingdom of God. During that time my Father showed me that the only way to change people's hearts is through love and sacrifice. There is no greater love than one who lays down one's life for another."

*Give me the strength to stay close to you, Lord.
Show me how to sacrifice myself for you.*

REFLECTION: How often do I fast and pray for God's guidance?

FEAR NO EVIL

"Even though I walk through the valley of the shadow of death, I will fear no evil, for you are with me."

PSALM 23:4

In my vision I saw myself walking in a dark forest with tall trees all around me. "My child, the world situation now is like a jungle. Everyone does whatever pleases oneself. Only a few follow me and walk in the light. Do not be afraid. As long as you hold my hand even though you are now in the dark valley I will protect and guide you every step of the way. Do not look back. Stay on course and you will see the light at the end of the tunnel. Trust in me 100% and know that I will walk with you day and night. Have no fear for I am always with you."

Lord Jesus, you are my good shepherd.
I know you will protect me from all evil.
Help me to be focused on you always.

REFLECTION: Do I trust that Jesus will be protecting me from all evil no matter where I am?

CUP OF WATER

> *"Anyone who gives you a cup of water to*
> *drink because you belong to Christ, amen, I*
> *say to you, will surely not lose his reward."*
>
> MARK 9:41

In my vision I saw Jesus healing a blind beggar who was sitting by the roadside. "My precious one, every good deed you do to the least of your brethren you do it to me. I will bless you and reward you a hundred fold. Do not ignore those around you who need your help. Give generously and give with love and compassion. You will be compensated in return. It will pay for your many sins when you spread your love and kindness to others. Let not one day go by without doing good to others. Your heart will be filled with my joy and peace and your reward will be great in heaven."

> *Thank you, Jesus, for your words of*
> *encouragement. I will try my best to*
> *do good every day of my life.*

REFLECTION: When was the last time I gave a cup of water to someone to drink?

WASH YOURSELVES CLEAN

"Wash yourselves clean! Put away your misdeeds from before my eyes; cease doing evil; learn to do good."

Isaiah 1:16-17

In my vision I saw myself kneeling down next to a pool by the temple washing my eyes and my face with the healing water. "My little one, unless you wash clean your eyes you will not see clearly the misdeeds that you do each day. Many people have blind spots concerning their own behavior. But they can see clearly their neighbor's sins. First wash yourself clean and change your ways before you correct others. Be compassionate and merciful to others and you will receive mercy from my Father. Love others as I have loved you.

Merciful Jesus, wash me clean with your living water. Help me to avoid doing evil but learn to be more loving towards others.

REFLECTION: Do I have blind spots that only see faults in others and not my own?

TRANSFIGURED

*"He was transfigured before them, and
his clothes became dazzling white, such as
no fuller on earth could bleach them."*

MARK 9:2-3

In my vision I saw resurrected Jesus all aglow and dressed in white with radiant light. "My child, yes, I have resurrected and my body has transfigured from earthly body to resurrected body. One day you, too, will have a similar body filled with light. Anyone who believes in me and keeps my commandments will live in heaven with me for eternity. You will be filled with joy and peace. You will see everything with your new eyes. You will see angels and saints. They will welcome you with open arms. I will come to bring you to my Father's house where I have prepared a place especially for you."

*My sweet Jesus, thank you for letting me know
that one day I will see you face to face. What joy
that will be! I can hardly wait to be in your arms.*

REFLECTION: Do I believe that one day my body will be transformed like Jesus' resurrected body?

STOP JUDGING

"Stop judging and you will not be judged. Stop condemning and will not be condemned."

LUKE 6:37

In my vision I saw a person pointing his finger at another who was distraught. "My beloved, leave the judging to me. Your job is to love and to forgive. For no one is perfect. Everyone has committed sins. So be kind and understanding as my Father is with you. He has forgiven you so many times. He let you repent and learn from your own mistakes. He has pardoned all your sins. Shall you not do the same for others? The more you forgive the more you will be forgiven. When you are filled with love for others you will have more compassion for them. Love conquers all evil."

Fill me, O Lord, with more of your love and compassion. Let me never judge or condemn others because only you are our judge.

REFLECTION: How often have I judged others unkindly and forgotten that Jesus is the one and only Judge?

MUCH PEACE

"Lovers of your law have much peace;
for them there is no stumbling block."

PSALM 119:165

In my vision I saw myself sitting on a bench by the bay. A sailboat went gently by in front of me. I felt such peace. "My loving child, when you follow my law your life will go as smoothly as the sailboat. You will be able to enjoy the ride without any trouble. But when you do not obey my law, your life will be full of storms, trials and tribulations. You will be filled with anxiety and fear. Trust in me and study my commandments day and night. My law is the blueprint for you every day. When you walk in my ways you will have a peaceful life that will glorify me. May my peace reign in your heart."

Lord Jesus, you are my Prince of Peace.
Come and dwell in my heart.

REFLECTION: Do I try my best to follow God's law and commandments and have peace in my life?

LIKE A CHILD

"Amen, I say to you, whoever does not accept the kingdom of God like a child will not enter it."

MARK 10:15

In my vision I saw a little child standing and admiring all the stars in the sky with awe and wonder. "My child, if you only realize how beautiful and awesome the kingdom of God is you will be like that child in your vision. Only a child with his pure heart will be able to see the beauty and wonder of my creation. Your eyes will be opened and you will know me and appreciate me even more. You will want to spend time alone with me and learn from me. For I am the truth and the light. I will fill your heart with awe and wonder. You will be able to grow closer to me daily."

O loving Jesus, teach me to love you more and more each day. Give me a pure heart like a child.

REFLECTION: Do I believe like a child what Jesus taught us about the Kingdom of God?

YOUR SINS

"Though your sins be like scarlet, they
may become white as snow."

ISAIAH 1:18

In my vision I saw myself holding a dirty heart in my hands. It was covered with mud. First Jesus poured his living water and cleaned my heart. After he restored it to its original condition, he poured his precious blood and made it full of life again. "My precious one, every time you confess your sins this is what happens. I will remove all your sins and restore your heart to its original beauty. Keep your heart pure and clean always. Fill it with love and gratitude. Pour your love and mercy on those who need them and your heart will be transformed."

Thank you, Jesus, for this beautiful vision.
Help me to keep my heart clean and fill
me with your love and compassion.

REFLECTION: Do I confess my sins to Jesus so that he can purify my heart with his precious blood?

MARCH

FAITHFUL FRIENDS

> *"Faithful friends are a sturdy shelter;*
> *whoever finds one finds a treasure."*
> SIRACH 6:14

In my vision I saw myself as a child holding hands with my best friend, skipping along on a street sidewalk giggling and laughing together. "My beloved, a good friend is a gift from God. Treasure your friends. They are hard to find. A faithful friend will be there to help you and to support you in time of need. I am your faithful friend. I hold you in the palm of my hand. I will always be there for you to protect you and to guide you. You can count on me. There is no greater love than what I have done for you on the cross. I am your best friend forever."

> *My loving Jesus, you are my best friend. I*
> *will always treasure you and adore you.*

REFLECTION: Who is my best friend? Is it Jesus or someone else?

PRODUCE ITS FRUITS

*"Therefore, I say to you, the Kingdom of
God will be taken away from you and given
to a people that will produce its fruits."*

MATTHEW 21:43

In my vision I saw a farmer sowing seeds in the field.
"My child, your job as my disciple is to sow God's words
to everyone you meet. Do not worry about the outcome.
I will pour my living water upon them and my light
will shine upon them to help them grow. Your job is to
spread the good news to everyone. Only in this way you
will produce much fruit. So go forth and do not be afraid
to share your faith with others. Anyone who hears my
word and believes in me will be saved. Rest assured that
your reward will be great in heaven. Preach the gospel
wherever you are and bring the souls back to me."

*My precious Jesus, I will go and spread your
good news to others. Give me the boldness to
speak your word without fear and hesitation.*

REFLECTION: Am I afraid to speak about Jesus and
bring the good news to others?

NOT WITH ME

"Whoever is not with me is against me, and
whoever does not gather with me scatters."

LUKE 11:23

In my vision I saw myself walking with Jesus and other disciples. We were talking and listening to Jesus. "My loving child, when you are with me, you will be filled with peace and joy. When you walk away from me you will be in darkness. For I am the light of the world. With me there is no darkness. I will show you the way to go and you will not be lost. You will be enlightened by my words and encouraged to do great things for my kingdom. I will teach you and show you everything. You will never walk alone when you are with me. I will never forsake you nor leave you. Be with me always."

Lord Jesus, I will follow you wherever
you lead me. Never let me be separated
away from you. You are all I need.

REFLECTION: Do I invite Jesus to go wherever I am going each day and ask for his guidance?

NEW CREATION

"Whoever is in Christ is a new creation;
the old things have passed away;
behold, new things have come."

2 CORINTHIANS 5:17

In my vision I saw a worm turned into a beautiful butterfly with colorful wings. "My loving child, when you live in me you will become a new creation, more beautiful than before. You will be able to fly and soar like the butterfly. Before you were bound in your own sinful ways and now you are set free. You are able to do great things because of me. You will be able to help others to become new creations too. Just go and tell them what I have done for you and they too will be transformed and set free. Let them know that they are my children also and precious in my sight."

Jesus Christ, Son of the living God, you
are my healer and my savior. Thank
you for giving me a new life.

REFLECTION: Have I changed my ways so that I am now a new creation in God's eyes?

DISOBEDIENCE

"For just as through the disobedience of the one person the many were made sinners, so, through the obedience of the one, the many will be made righteous."

ROMANS 5:19

In my vision I saw a student being punished by his teacher because of his disobedience. "My child, every action has consequences. Every act of disobedience will cause much pain and needs to be repented. Through disobedience of Adam and Eve, you are all punished and banished from the Garden of Eden. But through my act of obedience to my Father on the cross all are saved and those who choose to follow me and obey the Ten Commandments will have eternal life. Without obedience one cannot enter into heaven. Remember that righteous acts bring salvation."

My Jesus, help me to be as obedient as you were to your heavenly Father. I want to do everything according to your divine will.

REFLECTION: How often have I been disobedient to God and forgotten to follow His divine will?

WHATEVER YOU DID

*"Amen, I say to you, whatever you did for one
of these least brothers of mine, you did for me."*

MATTHEW 25:40

In my vision I saw a woman washing a young child in a bathtub. "My faithful child, action speaks louder than words. Those people who only talk about the poor but never help them with their desperate situations will not inherit heaven. But those who give even a glass of water to those who are thirsty will be rewarded. I have no more hands and feet to serve anyone here on earth but yours. So whatever you do to the least of my people you are doing it for me. My heart always goes out to the cry of the poor. Go and do good in my name and your reward will be great in heaven."

*Lord, give me a compassionate and
generous heart. Let me be your hands and
feet to serve all those who are in need.*

REFLECTION: Am I willing to spend time and energy to help those who are less fortunate than myself?

ALL MY FEARS

*"I sought the Lord, and he answered me
and delivered me from all my fears."*

PSALM 34:5

In my vision Jesus was embracing me and all my fears and worries disappeared instantly. "My beloved child, come to me whenever you are fearful. I am your refuge and your shelter. You can find peace and serenity when you are with me. Do not focus on the problems and the trials that you are facing. But focus on the solution that I will reveal to you. I will give you the wisdom and the strength to overcome all difficult situations. You will be able to handle all the problems with me at your side. Remember that I am the Almighty God and nothing is impossible with me. Trust in me with all your heart."

*Thank you, my Lord, for your unending
love and assurance. Jesus, give me the
courage to overcome all my fears.*

REFLECTION: Is Jesus my refuge and my shelter when I am in trouble?

GUILT

"'I confess my transgression to the Lord,'
and you took away the guilt of my sin."

PSALM 32:5

In my vision I saw a woman crouching on the ground covering her face. All around her men stood ready to stone her to death. When Jesus looked at them, they all dropped their stones one by one and walked away. "My precious child, people might find you guilty but I have already forgiven you. I have died on the cross for all your sins. By my wounds you are healed from your guilt and shame. Stand up and know that you have been redeemed and saved. By my water and blood that gushed out of my side, you have been washed clean. You are set free. Your sins have been forgiven. Go in peace."

My loving Jesus, thank you for removing
all my guilt and shame. Help me to avoid
sin especially in times of temptation.

REFLECTION: How often do I confess my sins to Jesus so that he can remove my guilt and my shame?

LOVE THE LORD

> *"You shall love the Lord your God with all your heart, with all your soul, with all your mind, and with all your strength."*
>
> DEUTERONOMY 6:5

In my vision I saw a bright red and pulsating heart full of life. "My beloved, if you cherish me more than anyone or anything in your life you will be blessed abundantly. You will have everything in the right order. All those who put money, fame or power above me, their lives will be miserable at the end. For you are created to love me and others. Without love your life is meaningless. Those who do not have love in their hearts will feel lonely and depressed. Love gives purpose to live each day. Let love be the most important thing that you do for the rest of your life."

> *I love you, Lord. You are the reason that I live each day. Without you, life has no purpose nor meaning.*

REFLECTION: Do I love God with all my heart, my soul, my mind and my strength?

SPRING RAIN

> *"He will come to us like the rain, like*
> *spring rain that waters the earth."*
> HOSEA 6:3

In my vision I saw a person with an umbrella singing and dancing in the rain. "My child, when you feel my presence, your heart will sing with joy. Because I will refresh you with my living water. Without me you will not find joy in this life. With me everything is possible. So wake up every morning and smell the roses and count your blessings. Sing with joy in your heart. Sing with gratitude and praise. This is the day the Lord has made, rejoice and be glad. As you drink my living water, your heart and your mind will be renewed and rejuvenated. Drink and be filled with my love and blessing."

> *My loving Jesus, my soul thirsts for you.*
> *Fill me with your living water so that I will*
> *grow more and more in love with you.*

REFLECTION: Do I wake up each morning praising and thanking Jesus for all that he has done for me?

LIVES THE TRUTH

"Whoever lives the truth comes to the light, so that his works may be clearly seen as done in God."

JOHN 3:21

In my vision I saw a monk sitting at his desk writing and copying the scripture. "My beloved, if you know my word then you will live in the truth. Read my word and study it, memorize it, write it and speak it to others. In this way my word will become powerful in whatever you do for others. It will bear much fruit and produce results more than you can ever imagine. Live each day proclaiming my word to others. This is the will of my Father. This is the way to build my kingdom. My word will enlighten your mind and everyone who accepts the truth will accept me into their hearts."

Yes, I will go and proclaim the truth to others. My loving Jesus, help me to have the courage to speak about you to others always.

REFLECTION: Do I read the Bible and study God's words, and meditate them in my heart daily?

HUMBLES HIMSELF

*"Whoever exalts himself will be humbled; but
whoever humbles himself will be exalted."*

MATTHEW 23:12

In my vision Jesus was carrying his cross and falling down three times. "My precious one, anyone who suffers for doing my Father's will will be exalted. Do not be discouraged but be persistent in your daily walk with me. When you fall and stumble, I will be there to help you get up and continue your journey. Be humble as I am humble. The more you humble yourself the more you will be exalted. Those who are prideful will be easily tempted to be self-sufficient. Lean on me and call for my help always. Remember that without me you can do nothing. But when you are with me all things are possible."

*Loving and gentle Jesus, make my heart
like yours, humble and merciful. Walk with
me for I need you always by my side.*

REFLECTION: Is it difficult for me to be humble and meek towards others?

CONTRITE SPIRIT

"My sacrifice, O God, is a contrite spirit; a contrite, humbled heart, O God, you will not scorn."

PSALM 51:19

In my vision I saw the King of Nineveh remove his robe and cover himself with sackcloth and sit in the ashes. "My love, whenever you repent from your sins, the angels in heaven will rejoice over you. Because only a humbled and contrite heart can enter into my kingdom. The number one sin is pride and disobedience. Anyone who confess his sins to me will be forgiven. It is better than a thousand sacrifices. No sin is too great for me to forgive. So do not hesitate to confess your sins and repent. I will wash you clean with my blood and water, and your soul will be as white as snow."

I am heartily sorry for having sinned against, Jesus. Thank you for washing me clean with your precious blood and water.

REFLECTION: Am I afraid to confess my sins to Jesus and to change my ways?

UNLESS I WASH YOU

*"Unless I wash you, you will have
no inheritance with me."*

JOHN 13:8

In my vision Jesus was kneeling down and washing Peter's feet. "My child, unless you are washed clean you cannot enter into my kingdom. Everyone is born with original sin. Only through baptism you are washed clean. The reason I washed my disciples' feet is to show you that you too must wash other people's feet and bring them to me so that they may be saved. Humility and service to others are two important virtues to have if you want to be my disciple. Now go and be ready to roll up your sleeves and serve one another as I have shown you."

*My Jesus, help me always be ready to serve you
and others. Give me a loving and serving heart.*

REFLECTION: Have I ever knelt down and washed someone's feet like Jesus did for his disciples?

CHANGED HIS MIND

> *"So the Lord changed his mind about*
> *the punishment he had threatened*
> *to inflict on his people."*
>
> EXODUS 32:14

In my vision I saw Moses kneeling in front of Mount Sinai praying and interceding for his people. "My beloved, you too can intercede for your family and friends. Bring all your concerns and worries to me. I hear your petitions. My heart is always moved when you call on me for help. Do not give up praying for them especially those who are lost. Pray and fast for those hearts that have turned away from me. I will bring them back. For I hear all your prayers. I will do what you ask of me. Pray constantly without ceasing. Pray from your heart and I will grant all your wishes."

> *O loving Jesus, thank you for always being there*
> *for me. You hear all my prayers and I know*
> *that you will answer them at the proper time.*

REFLECTION: How often do I pray and fast for others, especially those who are in need?

BROKENHEARTED

"The Lord is close to the brokenhearted; and those who are crushed in spirit he saves."

PSALM 34:19

In my vision I saw Jesus comforting a mother who just lost her son. "My loving child, blessed are those who mourn for they will be comforted. Come to me whenever your heart is broken and sad. I will bring hope and joy to your heart and blessings to your soul. Never suffer alone. For I care about you more than you can ever imagine. I know every hair on your head and when you sit or stand. I know what you are thinking before you speak. So trust in me when you are brokenhearted. I will be there to comfort you and to bring you out of sadness. Come now and put on your garment of joy."

Most precious Jesus, you are my comforter and my joy. I will turn to you and trust in you in times of sorrow. You are my healer and my redeemer.

REFLECTION: When I am brokenhearted, do I turn to Jesus and ask him to console me?

NEVER SEE DEATH

"Whoever keeps my word will never see death."

JOHN 8:52

In my vision I saw the empty tomb where they laid Jesus' body. "My child, death has no power over me. Remember how I have resurrected on Easter Sunday? I am the resurrection and the life. Whoever believes in me will never die. If you truly believe in my word, you too will live forever. My disciples and 500 people have seen my resurrected body. They know that they will live for eternity with me in heaven. That is why they were willing to lay down their lives for me. Unless a seed dies it will not bear much fruit. Remember your name is written in the Book of Life."

Yes, Lord Jesus, I will study your word
and keep it in my heart. Your word
is a lamp to my path to heaven.

REFLECTION: Do I truly believe that with Jesus I will have eternal life after death?

BE PERFECT

"Be perfect, just as your heavenly Father is perfect."

MATTHEW 5:48

In my vision I saw misty rain falling on green pasture and shortly afterwards a beautiful rainbow appeared over the land. "Beloved, my heavenly Father loves everyone on earth. His love for you is perfect. No one on earth can love you as much as He does. He cares about every detail of your life. He weeps when you are weeping. He rejoices when you are with Him. His arms are always open to receive you. Like a loving father He will carry you when you are too tired to go on living. So love one another as my Father loves you. This way you will be perfect in His sight."

Loving Jesus, thank you for revealing your Father's love for us. Enlarge my heart, Lord, so that I will be perfect as my heavenly Father is perfect.

REFLECTION: How can I be more perfect in God's eyes?

TRUST IN THE LORD

*"Blessed are those who trust in the
Lord; the Lord will be their trust."*

JEREMIAH 17:7

In my vision I saw a person holding on to a rock in a
white water river. He was clinging to it with his dear life.
"My child, as long as you are holding on to me you will
be saved. Even though there is raging water all around
you, you will not be drowned. For I will be with you
always. My rock is your solid foundation where you
can stand and trust. I will not abandon you nor forsake
you. Ever! For you are mine. I am your savior and your
redeemer. There is nothing to fear. Trust in me with all
your heart and I will bring you to safety and to eternal
life."

*My dear Jesus, you are my rock and my
salvation. I will always trust in you. Never
let me be separated away from you.*

REFLECTION: Do I trust Jesus with my whole heart,
especially when there is ragging water all around me?

I AM

> *"If you do not believe that I AM,*
> *you will die in your sins."*
>
> JOHN 8:24

In my vision I saw the universe with planets all moving in harmony around each other. "My precious one, I AM the living God who created this universe. Do you believe this? I created you with free will to choose me or not. If you do not believe that I AM the almighty God you will not be saved. Because I have created you to know me and to love me. Without me you can do nothing. If you believe in me you will surely worship me and love me. Those who do not believe in me are not capable to overcome their sins. Because of my cross you are saved. I have paid your ransom and set you free. So believe that I AM your savior and your redeemer and you will be saved."

> *Lord Jesus, I do believe that you are the son*
> *of the living God who has come to save me.*
> *Thank you for dying on the cross for my sins.*

REFLECTION: Am I sure that Jesus is the Son of the living God who will save me?

FORGIVE YOUR BROTHER

"So will my heavenly Father do to you, unless each of you forgives his brother from his heart."

MATTHEW 18:35

In my vision I saw two people hugging with each other. "My loving child, unless you forgive others from your heart you are like a sponge harboring poison in your bones. Unforgiveness brings bitterness and resentment and you will not be able to love from your heart -- because your heart will be closed. In order to receive love, you must first get rid of any anger and resentment towards others. Decide today to forgive everyone who has hurt you in the past. Ask God to forgive you for every time you have turned your back towards your brother. Then you will have peace and be able to love again."

Lord, please forgive me for all the times that I had bitterness and resentment towards others. Fill me with your peace and love.

REFLECTION: Have I forgiven all my brothers and sisters from my heart?

TO BE GREAT

> *"Whoever wishes to be great among you shall be your servant; whoever wishes to be first among you shall be your slave."*
>
> MATTHEW 20:26-27

In my vision I saw Mary went in haste to help her cousin Elizabeth in her sixth month of pregnancy. "My child, if you want to be great then you too must be a servant like Mary. The more you do for others the more treasure you will store up in heaven. My Father who is in heaven will be glorified through your good works. So do not let one day pass by without doing a good deed for others. It is in serving that you will receive. It is in giving that you will be great in God's eyes. This is your mission and your purpose in life. You are born to serve and to make a difference in people's lives."

O loving Jesus, I will go and serve others as Mary did. May you be glorified forever and ever, Amen.

REFLECTION: Do I go out of my way to be a servant to others as Jesus did?

LISTEN TO MY VOICE

> *"Listen to my voice, then I will be your*
> *God and you shall be my people."*
>
> JEREMIAH 7:23

In my vision I saw Jesus calling his sheep to follow him. "My precious one, stay close to me so that you can hear my voice. Do not wander far from me so that you might be lost. Only those who follow me and my commandments will hear my voice. When I speak, listen attentively. All the people who do not take time to be quiet will not be able to hear my voice. They are too occupied doing their own thing. To do my will, you must first listen to me. Without listening to my voice you can easily be misled by the evil one. Come closer to me and listen to my voice."

> *Speak, Lord, your servant is listening.*
> *Tell me what I should do each day. I only*
> *want to please you and to do your will.*

REFLECTION: Do I try to listen to Jesus' voice in the silence of my heart daily?

JESUS MET THEM

*"And behold, Jesus met them on
the way and greeted them."*
<small>MATTHEW 28:9</small>

In my vision I saw myself walking and Jesus came next to me and asked me how my day was. "My beloved, I am always walking next to you. I care everything about you and want to help you on your journey. Always remember that you do not travel alone. I am watching and guiding you. I will lead you on the right path and will protect you from all harm. Look for me wherever you go and I will be there for you. I know everything about you. I know what is in your heart and where you are going. Invite me to walk with you every day and you will never get lost. I am the way, the truth and the life."

*Thank you, Jesus, for always being next
to me no matter where I am going.
Lead me, Lord, to the right path.*

REFLECTION: Am I aware that Jesus is always walking by my side no matter where I am going?

WELL-TRAINED TONGUE

"The Lord God has given me a well-trained tongue that I might know how to speak to the weary."

ISAIAH 50:4

In my vision I saw Paul speaking in the marketplace and people were stopping to listen to him. "My child, you too are given a well-trained tongue. You have the qualifications to proclaim the good news to others. So do not be afraid to go and speak to them about your own conversion story. Tell them what I have done for you. Tell them how much I love them. Do not worry about what you are to say. For I will send the Holy Spirit upon you and you will speak the words that will move their hearts. You will open their ears to hear and they will know what an awesome God I am."

My loving Jesus, use me and mold me into your image and likeness. I want to be a faithful servant like Paul -- always ready to share faith with others.

REFLECTION: Do I trust that the Holy Spirit will give me the right words to proclaim the good news to others?

SINNERS

"God proves his love for us in that when we were still sinners Christ died for us."

ROMANS 5:8

In my vision Jesus was praying to his Father to forgive us from our sins while he was hanging on the cross. "My loving child, never doubt that I love you. I died a painful death on the cross for all your sins. Remember that I came into the world to save and not to condemn. All you need to do is to repent and ask for forgiveness and all your sins will be wiped clean by my precious blood. There is no sin too great for me to forgive. So do not be like Judas who hung himself. If he came and asked for forgiveness I would have forgiven him. So return to me every time when you have sinned."

Precious Jesus, thank you so much for dying and suffering on the cross for my sins. You are truly my savior and my redeemer.

REFLECTION: Do I realize that Jesus has died on the cross for all my sins?

GREAT MERCY

*"Do not put us to shame, but deal with
us in your kindness and great mercy."*

DANIEL 3:41-42

In my vision I saw a prostitute ready to be stoned to death. "My child, no matter how serious you have sinned do not turn your back against me. Come to me with your repentant heart. I will always have mercy on you. Do not get angry with yourself but to turn away from your sinful ways, come and follow me. I will wipe away all your tears and remove your guilt and shame. I will restore your heart of stone back to a heart of flesh. Be encouraged and be faithful to my commandments. Only in this way you will be set free. Have mercy on all those who have offended you as I have done for you."

*Lord Jesus, have mercy on me, a sinner.
Help me to be more merciful and kind
to others as you have been to me.*

REFLECTION: Do I have confidence in Jesus that he will be merciful to me no matter how sinful I have been?

OPENED MY EAR

> *"The Lord God opened my ear; I did
> not refuse, did not turn away."*
>
> ISAIAH 50:5

In my vision I saw a person sitting on top of a mountain listening to the wind and admiring the beautiful scenery with awe. "My beloved, when you spend time alone with me your ears will be opened and your heart will be filled with awe. It will be a mountain top experience. Come alone to a deserted place with me every day and your life will never be the same again. You will hear the birds singing and the leaves blowing like you have never experienced before. Come to seek me and you will find me. Your heart will be filled with love and peace. For I love you with an everlasting love."

> *Yes, my sweet Jesus, I love to hear your voice
> and your words of wisdom. Each morning I
> look forward to spend the time alone with you.*

REFLECTION: How often do I open my ears and try to listen to Jesus in my solitude?

EAT THIS BREAD

"As often as you eat this bread and drink the cup,
you proclaim the death of the Lord until he comes."

1 CORINTHIANS 11:26

In my vision I saw myself going up to receive communion. The minute the host touched my tongue my whole body became aglow with radiant light. "My precious one, this is what happens when you receive my body and my blood. I am in you and dwell within you. My light shines through you. Even though you cannot see it, this is what actually happens whenever you receive me. I treasure every moment you spend with me, adoring me and worshiping me. Tell me how much you love me. Come and eat my body and drink my blood often. I will give you everlasting life."

Precious Jesus, I love to receive your body and
blood every day. You are all I want and need.

REFLECTION: Do I hunger and thirst to receive the body and the blood of Jesus?

HE WAS PIERCED

"He was pierced for our offenses, crushed for our sins, upon him was the chastisement that makes us whole, by his stripes we were healed."

ISAIAH 53:5

In my vision I saw a soldier piercing Jesus' side and the blood and water flowed out. "My beloved, I gave myself totally for you and for your sins, even to my last drop of blood. For you I have suffered all the scourging and beating. For you are worth it. I willingly laid down my life for you, because I want you to spend eternity with me in heaven. I am your loving God. You are my joy and my precious possession. I treasure you above all else. Any time when you love me and others you bring me more joy than you can ever imagine."

My loving Jesus, thank you from the bottom of my heart for all the suffering and pain that you have endured on the cross for me. I am yours, Lord!

REFLECTION: Do I realize how much Jesus has suffered for my sins on the cross?

RESURRECTION OF LIFE

"Those who have done good deeds to the
resurrection of life, but those who have done
wicked deeds to the resurrection of condemnation."

JOHN 5:29

In my vision I saw Jesus rising into the sky while his disciples looked on with awe. "My child, one day you will also be resurrected into heaven. For you have done many good deeds while you are alive. Those who do wicked deeds will be condemned for eternity. Do not waste one day without doing at least one good deed. That is the reason you are created. Share your joy and hope with others. Tell them the good news about me. In this way you are helping me to bring others into heaven. Many have lost hope and forgot the true purpose of their lives. Go forth and help them to do good deeds each day."

Jesus, you are the resurrection and the life.
I will try my best to do as many good deeds
as I can each day for your glory, Lord.

REFLECTION: Have I tried to do at least one good deed per day for the honor and glory of God?

APRIL

LOVE YOUR NEIGHBOR

*"To love your neighbor as yourself is worth
more than burnt offerings and sacrifices."*

MARK 12:33

In my vision I saw Mary went in haste to help her cousin
Elizabeth who was pregnant. "My loving child, whatever you do to your neighbor you are doing it to me. For
I love everyone in this world. I died on the cross for all
of you. There is no exception. So when you do good to
others do not pick and choose who you are going to help
and be kind to. Treat everyone as if you would treat me.
Be loving and kind to every one as you want to lavish
your love upon me. Then your reward will be great in
heaven. Now go and love your neighbor as I love you."

*O loving Jesus, enlarge my heart to love you
and my neighbors as you have loved me.
May all my actions glorify and praise you.*

REFLECTION: Do I love everyone as Jesus loves me,
no matter whether he is rich or poor, young or old?

ILLNESS

> *"This illness is not to end in death,*
> *but is for the glory of God, that Son of*
> *God may be glorified through it."*
>
> JOHN 11:4

In my vision I saw Lazarus walking out of the tomb still wrapped in a cloth. "My child, I can make all illness and suffering into health and life again. For I made all things good even those seemed evil in men's eyes. Through suffering we can bring glory to God. In Lazarus' case everyone who was there at the tomb believed that I am the resurrection and the life. If you believe in me, you will have life after death. Illness and death is not the end but the beginning of your journey to heaven. Give thanks always even when you are suffering with illness. For through suffering you are glorifying my Father."

> *Yes, Lord Jesus, I do believe that you are*
> *the resurrection and the life. Through each*
> *illness you have brought me closer to you.*

REFLECTION: Do I give thanks to God when I am suffering from my illness or difficult times?

COMFORTS HIS PEOPLE

"The Lord comforts his people and
shows mercy to his afflicted."

ISAIAH 49:13

In my vision I saw a child crying on his mother's lap. "My dearest child, I will never leave you nor forsake you. I will always be there to comfort you in times of affliction. I love you with an everlasting love. You can come to me when you are in trouble. I will sooth your fear and anxiety and take away all your pain and worry. I will hold my arms around you until you feel safe and secure. You are never alone. My eyes are always upon you. I know when you sit or stand. I will never abandon you in times of need. I am your rock and your merciful savior."

Thank you for your words of comfort and
mercy. You are my God and my Lord.
I will always go to you for comfort.

REFLECTION: Do I believe that Jesus will always comfort me, especially when I need him most?

FILLED WITH AMAZEMENT

> *"When all the people saw him walking and praising God, they recognized him as the one who used to sit begging at the Beautiful Gate of the temple, and they were filled with amazement."*
>
> ACTS 3:9-10

In my vision I saw a blind man could see and a lame man could walk. Everyone around them was amazed. "My beloved, you too have the power to lay hands on people for healing when you pray in my name. Have faith in me. Pray with expectant faith. Like my disciples they know that alone they can do nothing. But with me all things are possible. Even the dead will rise and walk again. I am commissioning you to go out and proclaim the good news, heal the sick and raise the dead. Go with confidence in me. Know that I will be with you whenever you call on my name."

Lord Jesus, you are our healer and our savior. Give me the confidence and the boldness to step out of my comfort zone and go forth to do your will.

REFLECTION: Do I have the expectant faith in Jesus to heal the sick when I call on his name?

COMMUNITY OF BELIEVERS

> *"The community of believers was of one heart and mind, and no one claimed that any of his possessions was his own, but they had everything in common."*
>
> ACTS 4:32

In my vision I saw people bringing their money and treasure to Peter and sharing all that they have with others. "My beloved, everything you have is given to you by my Father. So you must share your treasure with others too. Your time and money are not only for your own use, but for others who are in need. Be generous with everyone who comes to you for help. Do not let them go away empty handed. The more you give, the more you will receive. You reap what you sow. So share what you have and more will be given to you. Your cup will never run dry."

> *Help me to be as generous as you are, Lord. Open my heart to love everyone who is less fortunate than I am.*

REFLECTION: Am I generous in sharing my money and time with those who come to me for my assistance?

THE CHRIST

*"'This is truly the prophet.' Others
said, 'This is the Christ.'"*

JOHN 7:41-42

In my vision I saw Jesus standing in between Moses and
Elijah. His robe became dazzling white. "My beloved,
I am the Christ and the Son of the living God. Moses
brought the Ten Commandments down from the
mountain for the people to follow. Elijah prophesied
about the coming of Messiah. I am the fulfillment of the
law and the prophecy. I came into the world so that you
might be saved. Without me you cannot enter into my
kingdom. With me you will have eternal life, a life full
of hope and joy. I am the Christ, your savior and your
redeemer."

*O sweet Jesus, you are my Lord, my
savior and my redeemer. I believe that
you are the son of the almighty God.*

REFLECTION: Do I believe that Jesus is the Christ
who came to be my savior and my redeemer?

KNOW THE TRUTH

"If you remain in my word, you will truly be my disciple, and you will know the truth, and the truth will set you free."

JOHN 8:31-32

In my vision Jesus was sitting under a large tree teaching his disciples. They were all listening to him attentively. "My beloved child, if you listen to me you will also know the truth. What is the truth? The truth is that you are made in the image and likeness of God. You are loved by my Father more than you can imagine. He sent me into this world to suffer and die for you so that you will know the truth and be set free from all your sins. There is no one like you in this entire world. You are chosen to inherit everything from my Father. You are precious in His sight."

Lord Jesus, you are the truth, the way and the life. Thank you for coming into this world to set me free.

REFLECTION: Do I know that I am a child of God and will inherit everything from Him one day?

MY LOVE

*"Though the mountain leave their place and the
hills be shaken, my love shall never leave you."*

ISAIAH 54:10

In my vision I saw a mother holding her baby tightly in
her arms protecting him from danger with her dear life.
"My child, you can be sure that I will protect you like a
mother hen during any danger or disaster. You will be
sheltered under my eagle's wings. No evil one can snatch
you away from my arms. I will save you from all your
enemies. You can trust in me with your whole heart. I
will always love you and be there for you. You are my
precious child and I treasure you. I will never leave you
nor forsake you. My love for you will last forever and
ever."

*Most precious Jesus, you are my shelter and
my salvation. With you I have nothing to fear.
Thank you for all your loving care for me.*

REFLECTION: Am I 100% sure that Jesus loves me
and he will never leave me nor forsake me?

WE HAVE SINNED

"We have sinned in complaining against the Lord and you. Pray the Lord to take the serpents away from us."

NUMBERS 21:7

I my vision I saw people begging Moses to intercede for them. Many of their family members have died after being bitten by the serpents. "My precious child, come to me when you are in trouble. Do not complain about anything but pray and ask for my assistance. I will help you. When you realize that you have sinned, do not go away and beat yourself up. Come to me and confess your sins to me. I will wash you clean and will give you the grace to sin no more. I will strengthen you from all temptations. You will be saved if you repent from your heart. I am your merciful and forgiving God."

Lord Jesus, thank you for dying on the cross for all my sins. Please forgive me for the times when I have complained and sinned against you.

REFLECTION: Do I complain to God instead of trusting in His merciful love for me?

PIERCED MY HANDS

"They have pierced my hands and my feet; I can count all my bones."

PSALM 22:17-18

In my vision I was Jesus hanging on the cross between two criminals. His hands and feet were covered with blood. His face was disfigured by the crown of thorns. "My love, what I have suffered on the cross for you is more than words can describe. Every bone in my body ached from the whipping and scourging at the pillar. But most of all my heart was broken with sadness. Because so many people still are ignorant about my existence. They do not know how much I love them. I willingly died on the cross for each soul. If I have to be nailed again on the cross for one more soul I would be glad to do it again."

Most loving and adorable Jesus, I love you and thank you for all you have suffered for me. I will go and tell others about your great love for them.

REFLECTION: Can I visualize how much Jesus suffered on the cross just for the love of me?

SHARP-EDGED SWORD

"He made my mouth like a sharp-edged sword,
concealed me and shielded me by his hand."

ISAIAH 49:2

In my vision I saw a sword standing like a cross with brilliant light radiating from it. In the middle of it there was a red pulsating heart. "My beloved, I will use you like a two- edged sword and fill you with the Holy Spirit. The most important thing is your heart. It must be filled with my love. From your heart you will radiate my light and my salvation to others. Go forth and be a useful instrument of mine, loving each person and cutting them free from their sinful ways and removing their guilt and shame. I will protect you from all harm. I will hold you in the palm of my hands."

Lord Jesus, you are the light and the
salvation. Use me and hold me close to your
heart. Protect me from all my enemies.

REFLECTION: Is my mouth like a two-edge sword that Jesus can use to set the captives free?

COME TO MARY

> *"Many of the Jews who had come to Mary and seen what Jesus had done began to believe in him."*
>
> JOHN 11:45

In my vision I saw myself going to Mary. But she pointed me to go to Jesus. "My child, my mother will always bring every soul closer to me. She knows who I am. She never forgets that she is a creature created by God and I am the Son of the living God. She knows that anyone who comes to me will be saved. Anyone who goes to my mother she will gently lead them to me. She knows how much I love each one of you. For this reason I died on the cross for you. I love you with an everlasting love. Come to me and your faith will be increased a hundred fold."

> *Loving Jesus, I want to know you and love you more and more each day. Mary, my mother, pray for me always.*

REFLECTION: Have I ask Mary, the mother of God, to bring me closer to Jesus?

DO YOU LOVE ME

> *"'Simon, son of John, do you love me more*
> *than these?' Simon Peter answered him,*
> *'Yes, Lord, you know that I love you."*
>
> JOHN 21:15

In my vision I saw myself walking side by side with Jesus on a beach."My child, do you love me more than anyone else? Do you put me first in your life? Are you willing to go out and tell the good news about my salvation to everyone? Are you willing to sacrifice yourself for me? Do not be afraid that you will have to do everything on your own ability. No, I will be with you and walk with you till the end. You do not carry this mission alone. I will send people to help you. You need not be worried nor anxious about anything. You will be empowered by the Holy Spirit."

> *My Jesus I will go where you send me.*
> *I love you with my whole heart. With*
> *you by my side I will not be afraid.*

REFLECTION: Do I love Jesus so much that I want to tell others all about him?

INTO YOUR HANDS

"Jesus cried out in a loud voice, 'Father, into your hands I command my spirit' and when he had said this he breathed his last."

LUKE 23:46

In my vision I saw Jesus hanging on the cross crying out to his Father in heaven. "My loving child, live each moment as if today is your last day here on earth. Remember that your life here is limited. Spending each day doing God's will is the most important thing you can accomplish. Everything else is vanity. Ask me what I have planned for you to do at the beginning of each day. This way you will not be sidetracked. Offer every good deed for the glory of my Father and He will bless you abundantly. Be loving in everything you do and you will be blessed forever."

Loving Jesus, help me to live each day pleasing and glorifying God. I surrender myself to you every moment of my life.

REFLECTION: Do I spend each day doing God's will instead of my own?

PERFUMED OIL

*"Mary took a liter of costly perfumed oil made
from genuine aromatic nard and anointed the
feet of Jesus and dried them with her hair."*

JOHN 12:3

In my vision I saw all the disciples were surprised to
see Mary using such an expensive oil on Jesus' feet. "My
beloved, nothing can pay me back for all that I have
done for you. There is no one who love you more than
I do. The time you lavish your money, time and talents
on me is never wasted. The most loving thing that you
can do for me is to pour your love on those who need
me most. I have no more hands nor feet now but yours.
Every good deed and sacrifice you do is like pouring
costly perfumed oil over my feet. Every time when you
surrender yourself to my will is like anointing my feet."

*My most loving Jesus, teach me how to love
you as Mary did. Give me a generous heart so
that I will be able to lavish my love on others.*

REFLECTION: Am I willing to lavish my money, time
and talent for Jesus as Mary did?

WALKING ON THE SEA

*"When they had rowed about three or four miles,
they saw Jesus walking on the sea and coming
near the boat, and they began to be afraid."*

In my vision I saw Jesus walking on turbulent water towards Peter's boat. They were all terrified thinking it was a ghost. "My child, do not be afraid when everything around you is in chaos. I will be there with you in the storm. You have nothing to fear but trust in me. If you truly believe that I am the Son of the living God, then you should have no fear when you are with me. You know I will always protect you and guard you from all harm. Fear is not from me. Perfect love casts out all fear. So be assured that I am there for you especially when you need me most. Trust me with all your heart!"

*Sweet Jesus, I place my trust in you. Help
me to focus on you and remove all my
fear especially when I am in trouble.*

REFLECTION: Do I have the courage to step out of the boat and walk on water if Jesus asks me to?

BREAD OF GOD

*"For the bread of God is that which comes
down from heaven and gives life to the world."*

In my vision Jesus in his white garment descended from heaven and entered into the white host when a priest was elevating it at the altar. "My love, every time when the priest utters the words 'This is my body' during Mass the host becomes my real body and blood. Whoever eats my body and drinks my blood will have life everlasting. For my body is true food and my blood true drink. Even though your eyes cannot see my true presence, it is actually happening every time during the consecration. So come to receive me as often as you can. Let me nourish you and fill you with my love and presence. I will strengthen you and nourish you. Come to my feast."

*My Lord and my God, I need you and
long to receive your body and blood. Fill
me with your presence and never let
me be separated away from you.*

REFLECTION: Do I believe that the bread became the real body and blood of Jesus as he said at the last supper?

MY HELP

"The Lord is my help, therefore I am not disgraced; I have set my face like flint, knowing that I shall not be put to shame."

ISAIAH 50:7

In my vision Jesus was kneeling and praying in the olive garden while his disciples were all asleep nearby. His sweat became like drops of blood. An angel came to minister to him. "My precious child, when you go through trials and tribulations always remember that your angel is with you. He will comfort you and minister to you. You will never suffer alone. I will give you the strength to carry your cross. You will be able to endure to the end. You will have the courage to embrace all the suffering. Fear not, I am always with you. You can count on me and you will triumph at the end."

Merciful Jesus, thank you for your words of comfort. I will call on you whenever I am in trouble. My guardian angel be with me always.

REFLECTION: When I am in trouble do I realize that Jesus and my angel are always there to help me?

SEVERE PERSECUTION

"There broke out a severe persecution
of the church in Jerusalem, and all were
scattered throughout the countryside."

ACTS 8:1

In my vision I saw soldiers were going from house to house searching for Christians. "My beloved, do not worry about persecution. But stay close to me. This is a time of purification. Those who truly love me will follow me till the end. Remember all things work for good for those who love me. So have peace in your heart and know that I am in control. Have no anxiety whatsoever. As a result of the persecution Christians spread to all over the world. This all worked out as I have planned. So have complete faith in me and trust in my infinite wisdom. I will never abandon you to face the persecution alone."

Help me, O Lord, when I am under
persecution. Give me the courage to
trust in you in every situation.

REFLECTIONS: Do I have faith and trust in Jesus, especially when I am under trials and persecution?

SAVE THE WORLD

*"I did not come to condemn the
world but to save the world."*

JOHN 12:47

In my vision I saw a fisherman casting his net and catching many fish. "My child, I came into the world not to condemn but to save the world. I called my fishermen disciples to cast out their nets not only to catch fish but also to be fishers of men. Now I am calling you to be my disciple and to bring souls to me. My deepest desire is to save everyone. I am a compassionate and merciful God. Anyone who hears my voice and believes in me will be saved. Go now and spread my good news to everyone you meet each day. All those who hear my word and believe in me will be saved."

*Thank you, Jesus, for calling me to be
your disciple. Give me more grace and
courage to go out to do your will.*

REFLECTION: Is Jesus calling me to be a fisher of men and bring souls to him?

HOLY ONE

> *"We have come to believe and are convinced*
> *that you are the Holy One of God."*
>
> JOHN 6:69

In my vision I saw a resurrected Jesus with brilliant light radiating from his body. "My beloved child, do you believe that I am the Holy One sent by my Father to die on the cross for you? Come closer to me and you will see that I am the living bread that will nourish you on your journey towards my Father. I will strengthen you and lead you to heaven. No one has died on the cross, been resurrected and ascended into heaven except me. I am the resurrection and the life. If you believe in me you too will be in heaven with me one day. I am the living God who will give you everlasting life."

> *Yes, Lord Jesus, I do believe that you are*
> *the Holy One who reigns in heaven. I*
> *want to follow you always so that one day*
> *I will be united with you for eternity.*

REFLECTION: Do I believe that one day I will be united with the resurrected Jesus in heaven?

GOOD SHEPHERD

*"I am the good shepherd. A good shepherd
lays down his life for the sheep."*

JOHN 10:11

In my vision Jesus was tending his sheep in the green pasture. "My little one, to be a good shepherd one must be willing to lay down one's life for another. There are many Christians who are martyred because of their love for me. There are many parents who work day and night to support their families. These are just a few examples of a good shepherd. A good shepherd will never abandon his duty to protect his sheep. I am a good shepherd and I have laid down my life for you. You are my precious child. I will always protect you from all harm."

*Jesus, you are my good shepherd. I will
always follow you wherever you lead
me. Jesus, I place my trust in you.*

REFLECTION: Is Jesus my beloved shepherd who will always be with me protecting me and guiding me?

RISE FROM THE DEAD

"They did not yet understand the scripture
that he has to rise from the dead."

JOHN 20:9

In my vision Jesus was standing in front of Thomas and showing him his wounds in his hands. "My beloved child, do you believe that I am truly risen from the dead? Yes, it is true. More than five hundred people have seen me after my death on the cross. After I showed my wounds to Thomas, he quickly knelt down and said, 'My Lord and my God!' I had to die so that you will be saved from all your sins. Anyone who believes in me will have everlasting life. For I have paid the price to redeem you on the cross. Without me there is no resurrection. One day you too will have eternal life with me in heaven."

Most loving Jesus, I believe that one day
I will be with you in heaven for you have
redeemed me by your holy cross.

REFLECTION: Do I have faith in Jesus that he has truly risen from the dead?

THE GATE

*"I am the gate. Whoever enters through
me will be saved, and will come in
and go out and find pasture."*

JOHN 10:9

In my vision I saw a large pearly gate that leads into
heaven. "My child, I am the way, the truth and the life.
If you know me and follow my commandments you will
go through the gate one day and enter into heaven. The
pearls on the gate are the seeds of wisdom. You need to
be wise and choose to follow me instead of the world.
To know me is to gain everything your heart is seeking.
I am your treasure. I am the gate that will lead you to
joy and peace. Seek me first and everything else will be
given to you. Come my precious one. Come to my gate
and you will have eternal rest."

*O precious Jesus, you are my gate and my
savior. Lead me into your heart and never
let me be separated away from you.*

REFLECTION: Do I look forward to entering the gate
so that I will be united with Jesus forever?

IN MY NAME

> *"If you ask anything of me in*
> *my name, I will do it."*
> JOHN 14:14

In my vision I saw Jesus laying his hands on the children. "My little one, can a mother who loves her child refuse to give him whatever he asks of her? No. Unless it is bad for the child. So it is when you ask my Father in my name. He cannot refuse you. Because my Father loves you as much as I love you. He will not refuse you unless he has something better for you. He knows you as well as I know you. My Father and I are one. Whatever you ask in my name I will surely give you. I love you with an everlasting love. I will always answer your prayers. Ask and you shall receive."

> *My sweet Jesus, you are King of kings and Lord*
> *of lords. Thank you for always answering my*
> *prayers. May your name be praised forever!*

REFLECTION: How often do I pray in the name of Jesus and expect that he will answer my prayers?

SUFFER AND RISE

*"Thus it is written that the Christ would suffer
and rise from the dead on the third day and that
repentance, for the forgiveness of sins, would
be preached in his name to all the nations."*

LUKE 24:46-47

In my vision I saw Jesus radiant with bright light coming out of his tomb. "My child, death has no more power over me nor you. If you believe in me, you too will live forever. You will spend eternity with me and my Father. First, you must repent from all your sins and confess them from your heart. I will wash you clean with my blood and water. Only then you will be ready to go forth like my disciples to preach the good news to all the nations. Do not be afraid. Take courage and be bold. May my kingdom come on earth as it is in heaven."

*Thank you, Jesus, for suffering and dying
on the cross for my sins. I will go forth
to spread your gospel to everyone.*

REFLECTION: Do I believe that Jesus really rose from the dead after suffering and dying on the cross?

GOD RAISED HIM

*"God raised him from the dead, and for many
days he appeared to those who had come
up with him from Galilee to Jerusalem."*

ACTS 13:30-31

In my vision I saw a beautiful and colorful hot air balloon going up into the sky. "My precious child, yes, God raised me from the tomb as He has promised. One day you too will be raised. On that day I will come and bring you to heaven to meet my Father face to face. You will be filled with love, peace and joy. I have prepared a place just for you. You need not fear nor worry. I will send angels to lead you there. You will be with your love ones who have gone before you. The saints will come to welcome you. It will be a day of rejoicing where there be no more tears nor sorrow."

*How I long for that day, my precious
Jesus, when I will be with you forever in
the presence of your Father. My heart is
filled with joy just thinking about it.*

REFLECTION: Do I look forward to the day when I will be united with Jesus and all my loved ones in heaven?

FIVE THOUSAND

> *"Many of those who heard the word
> came to believe and the number of men
> grew to about five thousand."*
>
> ACTS 4:4

In my vision I saw a man on stage throwing hundred dollar bills to a large audience. Many people in the audience reached out to catch the money and were filled with joy. "My beloved, I will supply the word and all you need to do is to spread it to others. Those who receive my word will be converted and saved. Your job is to give it away everywhere you go. For my word has power to heal and to save. See how my disciples were transformed after they were filled with the Holy Spirit; they were able to go out and convert five thousand people afterwards."

> *Yes, Lord Jesus, I will go and spread
> your word to everyone I meet each day.
> Fill me with your Holy Spirit.*

REFLECTION: Am I ready to go out and spread God's word to others so that they too may be converted and saved?

FRIENDS

"I have called you friends, because I have told
you everything I have heard from my Father."

JOHN 15:15

In my vision Jesus was sitting across from me and we were enjoying a dinner together. "My friend, I know everything about you. You know how much I love you and it was I who chose you to be my disciple. You were called from the day you were baptized. You carry me in your heart every time you receive me in the communion. You have confidence in me and you trust me. I chose you because you are loving and generous with everyone. You are willing to listen and to carry out my wishes. You are truly my friend. I will never forget you nor leave you. You can count on me."

Thank you, Jesus, for being my friend. I
treasure you above everyone else. I know how
much you love me and care about me.

REFLECTION: Is Jesus my true friend who has told me everything that I need to know about him?

KEEP MY WORD

"Whoever loves me will keep my word, and my Father will love him, and we will come to him and make our dwelling with him."

JOHN 14:23

In my vision I saw Jesus teaching me under a large tree. "My beloved, it is true, when you keep my word my Father will love you. My Father and I are one. Whoever loves me will also love my Father. Whoever honors me will also honor my Father. When you keep my word, your life will be changed. You will no longer desire the things in this world. You will treasure my teachings and follow my laws. You will be able to do mighty deeds in my name. So keep my word and study scripture daily. Only in this way you will be transformed into my image and likeness."

Lord Jesus, you have the word of everlasting life. I will study and learn from your word in the scripture day and night.

REFLECTION: Do I keep Jesus' words in my heart and follow his teachings and commandments?

MAY

MANY DWELLING PLACES

"In my Father's house there are
many dwelling places."
JOHN 14:2

In my vision I saw a picture of the universe that was never ending. "My child, where my Father lives you will be there one day too. I am preparing a place for you in my Father's house. Do not be concerned with what it will look like or how you will get there. Because I am the way, the truth and the life. I came to lead you there. You will be on the right path to eternal bliss. Follow my footsteps one day at a time. Live each day with love, joy and peace in your heart. Consecrate yourself, your family and loved ones to me. Soon you will all be united together in a place there I have prepared for you."

Thank you, Jesus, for your assurance that
one day my family and loved ones will all
be dwelling in your Father's house.

REFLECTION: Have I consecrated myself, my family and my loved ones to Jesus?

WORTHY TO SUFFER

"So they left the presence of the Sanhedrin,
rejoicing that they had been found worthy to
suffer dishonor for the sake of the name."

ACTS 5:41

In my first vision I saw Jesus being whipped at the pillar. The second vision Jesus was spat upon by the soldiers and they put a thorny crown upon his head. The third vision Jesus was nailed on the cross. "My precious child, there is no greater love than what I have done for you. Are you willing to suffer in my name? Are you willing to die yourself in order to build my kingdom? There is no greater love than one who lays down his life for another. God is love. When you do anything in love, you are imitating me. Come and follow me."

My dear Jesus, thank you for suffering so
much in order to set me free from eternal
damnation. Help me to have courage to
suffer for others as you did for me.

REFLECTION: Am I willing to suffer and lay down my life for the love of Jesus?

DO THE WORKS

> *"Amen, amen, I say to you, whoever believes in*
> *me will do the works that I do, and will do greater*
> *ones than these, because I am going to the Father."*
>
> JOHN 14:12

In my vision I saw the disciples collecting the leftover bread and fish in their twelve baskets. "My beloved, you will be like my disciples if you do what I tell you to do. You will be collecting more blessings than you ever thought possible. For I am a generous God and I will shower you with miracles like I did when I was with my apostles. They were equipped to go out and perform miracles like I did. They had power to heal and to bind the evil spirits. Never be fearful that you will be left alone powerless. For I am always with you. Have confidence in me. Now go in peace."

> *Loving Jesus, help me to trust you every day of*
> *my life. I believe that all things are possible with*
> *you. Here I am, Lord, I come to do your will.*

REFLECTION: Do I have the courage to go out and do the works that Jesus has asked me to do?

PRAISE THE LORD

"Praise the Lord from the heavens;
praise him in the heights."

PSALM 148:1

In my vision I saw the man giving flowers to a grateful lady. "My child, every time that you praise me is like lavishing me with flowers and gifts. It is the most precious gift that you can give me. So praise me all day long. When you praise it is like honey on my lips and music to my ears. Praising me will give you joy and peace. There is nothing I desire more from you. The flowers praise me with their beautiful colors and fragrance. The animals praise me by their majestic ways of roaring and jumping. Only you can praise me from your heart to my heart. Never cease praising me, my beloved one."

Jesus, I praise you and I adore you
from the bottom of my heart. May you
be glorified and honored forever.

REFLECTION: Do I remember to praise Jesus from my heart every day of my life?

PERSECUTED ME

"If they persecuted me, they will also persecute you."

JOHN 15:20

In my vision Jesus was standing in front of Pontius Pilot with his hands bound together and wearing a crown of thorns. "My love, this world does not know me nor the truth. They are living in sin. Do not follow what the world is saying. If you follow me you will live in the truth. The truth will set you free. Even though Pontius Pilot had my hands bound, in reality his life is the one that was in trouble. For I laid down my life willingly. But he was not free to make his own decision. So do not be afraid of the world. When you live in me you will know the truth. Be strong and stand firm in your faith."

Lord Jesus, be with me always. For I am weak and easily influenced by the world. Give me the wisdom and fortitude to withstand all persecution.

REFLECTION: If I am persecuted will I have the courage to stand firm in my faith?

ASK THE FATHER

"Amen, amen, I say to you, whatever you ask the Father in my name he will give you."

JOHN 16:23

In my vision I saw Jesus teaching his disciples how to pray the Our Father. "My beloved, the prayer I taught my disciples is the key on how to pray to my Father. First, praise His name and visualize Him sitting on his throne. Always ask in accordance to His will. Because He wants the best of everything for you in mind before you even open your mouth. He knows what your deepest desires and needs are. He will provide all that is essential for you to live a happy and peaceful life. But first you must forgive everyone from your heart. Then, whatever you ask in my name He will give it to you."

Thank you, Jesus, for giving us the Our Father prayer. I will ask the Father in your name from now on.

REFLECTION: Do I truly believe that when I pray in the name of Jesus my Father in heaven will answer me?

WE ARE SAVED

"We believe that we are saved through the grace of the Lord Jesus, in the same way as they."

ACTS 15:11

In my vision I saw many people trying to get hold of the life-savers that were thrown down from a big ship to save them from drowning. "My child, I am the savior of the world. Anyone who comes to me will receive grace and salvation. It is not through your own good deeds but through my grace that you will go to heaven. For without me you will not enter the Kingdom of God. Only those who love me and follow my commandments will have eternal life. It is by my cross that you are saved. Have faith in me and I will bring you to my Father's house."

Precious Jesus, pour your love and grace upon me so that I will be saved and able to spend eternity with you in heaven. I believe that you are the savior of the world.

REFLECTION: Do I have faith in Jesus that he will pour his grace upon me so that I will be saved through him?

LOVE ONE ANOTHER

"This is my commandment: love
one another as I love you."

JOHN 15:12

In my vision I saw a row of ladies linking arms dancing together and singing in unison. "My precious one, nothing pleases me more than to see all my children being united and loving each other. My Father's greatest desire is that all His children love each other as He loves me. I have suffered and sacrificed myself on the cross to show you how to really love others. It warms my heart to know that you are following my example and obeying my commandments. Now go and love one another as I have loved you. Your reward will be great in heaven."

Yes, my beloved Jesus, I will try to love
everyone as you love me. All I want is to
please you and your Father in heaven.

REFLECTION: Is there someone in my life that I have a problem loving?

REMAIN IN ME

"Whoever eats my flesh and drinks my
blood remains in me and I in him."

JOHN 6:56

In my vision I saw a man being chained to his body-guard. "My child, every time when you go and receive my body and my blood, we become one. Our bond is even stronger than the chain in your vision. We are united in body, mind and soul. The more you receive me the more you will become like me. Your thoughts will be my thoughts. Your prayers will be my prayers. Your actions will be according to my will. So come to receive communion often. There is no greater food to nourish you than the Eucharist. Remain in me and I will remain in you."

Lord Jesus, to receive your flesh and
blood is the highlight of my day. Thank
you for this most precious gift.

REFLECTION: How often do I go and receive the communion and be united with Christ in body, mind and soul?

TAKE COURAGE

*"In the world you will have trouble, but take
courage. I have conquered the world."*

JOHN 16:33

In my vision I saw Jesus riding on a white horse leading
an army behind him. When the enemies saw his light
they all fled. "My loving child, the battle is already won.
You have nothing to fear if you walk and follow me. You
will be protected and the enemy will not be able to attack
you. Those who follow me will be safe and those who go
ahead of me will perish. When you stand behind me I
will make you invisible to the enemy. But when you go
forth alone you will be in danger. Stay close to me and
call on me when you are in trouble. I will never leave you
nor forsake you."

*Loving Jesus, I will follow you always. You are my
rock and my savior, my shelter and my fortress.*

REFLECTION: Do I have the courage to follow Jesus
in everything I do?

GO ON SPEAKING

*"Do not be afraid. Go on speaking and
do not be silent, for I am with you."*

ACTS 18:9-10

In my vision Jesus was speaking to thousands of people who were listening attentively to him. "My beloved, your job is to proclaim the good news to others. Do not be afraid. I will give you the right words to say that will touch their hearts. I need you to spread the news to everyone you meet. My people are eager to hear the miracles and healings that you have seen and heard. When you share my stories with them it will give them hope and confidence that I am still here amongst you. Their lives will be filled with joy and hope. So continue to speak and do not be silent."

*Loving Jesus, you have the words of wisdom.
Give me the courage to be always ready to
share the miracles and healings with others.*

REFLECTION: When was the last time that I have shared the good news about Jesus with others?

WE ARE ONE

> *"I have given them the glory you gave me, so that they may be one, as we are one, I in them and you in me."*
>
> JOHN 17:22-23

In my vision I saw planets all revolving and turning around the center of the universe. "My child, when you align yourself to my will, you will also be in unison and harmony with the entire world. You will experience my peace beyond your understanding. You will have joy when you are united with my Father and me. You will know that we are in control and all will be well. Be one with me and with each other. It is the only way to live a peaceful and joyful life. Let love be the center of all you do each day. For God is love."

> *Heavenly Father, Son and the Holy Spirit, three persons in one God, be with me today and every day of my life. I want to be one with you.*

REFLECTION: Do I live a peaceful and joyful life knowing that I am united with my loving God?

HEAR MY VOICE

"My sheep hear my voice; I know them, and they follow me."

JOHN 10:27

In my vision I saw an old man holding a horn-like instrument next to his ear so that he could hear better. "My child, many people cannot hear my voice because there is too much noise around them and they have not made an effort to listen to me. The most important ingredient in listening is to be silent and be still. Only in silence your heart will be opened and your ears will be able to hear my soft voice within you like two lovers whispering in each other's ear. The closer you are with me, the better you will hear my voice and follow me."

Speak, Lord, your servant is listening. Your words are more precious to me than gold and silver.

REFLECTION: Do I take the time to be with Jesus alone in the silence of my heart so that I will be able to hear his voice?

HAVE FAITH

> *"Do not let your hearts be troubled. You*
> *have faith in God; have faith also in me."*
>
> JOHN 14:1

In my vision I was in a boat where a storm was raging all around me. "My loving child, if you realize that I am in the boat with you, you would not be afraid. You would have asked me for help. Remember, I am with you always no matter when and where you are and what kind of situation you are in. You need not be anxious about anything. Do you believe that I have power and authority over storms? Do you believe that I will save you whenever you are in trouble? Fear not. Everything is under my control. Have faith in me and you will be saved"

> *Thank you, Jesus, for your words of*
> *encouragement. With you at my side I*
> *will not fear but have faith in you.*

REFLECTION: Do I have the faith and trust in Jesus to rescue me when I am in the midst of a storm?

CONSECRATED

"I consecrate myself for them, so that they also may be consecrated in truth."

JOHN 17:19

In my vision I saw a person all dressed in white laying down on the floor with his face resting on the ground next to the altar. His hands were spread out like a cross. "My beloved, I am the way, the truth and the life. When you have consecrated yourself to me, you will be set apart and live a life in the truth. You will be following my way. You will know the truth and the truth will set you free. Live each day set apart from those who do not believe in the truth for they do not know me nor love me. It is your calling to reveal the truth to them."

My loving Jesus, I want to consecrate myself to you and follow you always. You are the way, the truth and the life.

REFLECTION: Have I consecrated myself to Jesus, to live a life in the truth like him?

MY PEACE

"Peace I leave with you; my peace I give to you.
Not as the world gives do I give it to you."

JOHN 14:27

In my vision I saw a child being cuddled in his mother's arms. "My precious one, with me you have nothing to fear but have peace knowing that no harm with hurt you. You are safe in my arms. Even though everything around you might be falling apart, you will still have peace knowing that I am in control. Every moment in your life is under my watchful eyes. For I love you more than you can ever imagine. Every hair on your head is counted. So have peace and joy in your heart. Place your complete trust in me and know that I will always protect you in my loving arms."

Jesus, thank you for your loving assurance.
Fill me with your peace so that I can
pass it to others around me.

REFLECTION: Do I feel peaceful and joyful knowing that I am always in the loving arms of Jesus?

SUBMIT YOURSELF

*"Submit yourselves to God. Resist the
devil and he will flee from you."*

JAMES 4:7

In my vision I saw a woman dancing tango with a gentleman wearing a formal tuxedo. "My child, when you submit a hundred percent to my will we will be one heart and one mind. The evil one will not be able to come near you. Like a couple dancing the Argentina tango together in your vision, the woman only moves when the man leads her. She never takes any step until he moves her. She is glued to him and nothing will separate her from him. They move as one. It is the same when you submit yourself to my will. Come and dance with me."

*My sweet Jesus, I love to dance with
you. Hold me tight and never let me
be separated away from you.*

REFLECTION: Am I united with Jesus in my mind and heart so that we can move together as one?

YOUR JOY

*"I have told you this so that my joy may be
in you and your joy may be complete."*

JOHN 15:11

In my vision I saw myself holding a beautiful bouquet of roses with a big smile on my face. "My beloved, you are joyful because you know in your heart how much I love you. When you know you are loved, your heart will sing with joy. Love is the most important thing in everyone's life. If you want to bring joy to others do everything with love. Love is what everyone is craving for. Without love life has no meaning. So remain in my love and your joy will be complete. Be filled with my joy and your life will never be the same again."

*Fill me, O Lord, with your love and
my joy will be complete. I love you and
I adore you with my whole heart.*

REFLECTION: Do I feel joyful knowing that Jesus will always love me no matter what?

PUFF OF SMOKE

> *"You have no idea what your life will be like tomorrow. You are a puff of smoke that appears briefly and then disappears."*
>
> JAMES 4:14

In my vision I saw Jesus sitting down with his disciples by the Sea of Galilee teaching them. "My faithful one, life is short. But remember that within the three short years that I spent with my disciples I was able to prepare them to build my church and my kingdom here on earth. Even though your life span is limited, you can still make a difference in other people's lives around you. Do not let one day go by without telling them about me nor neglecting to do good deeds for my glory and honor. Every day counts. With my help you will be able to move mountains."

Thank you, Jesus, for reminding me that my life is short here on earth. Help me to live each day doing your will.

REFLECTION: Do I try to do at least one good deed per day knowing how short our life here on earth is?

MORE BLESSED TO GIVE

"Keep in mind the words of the Lord Jesus who himself said, 'It is more blessed to give than to receive.'"

ACTS 20:35

In my vision Jesus was standing in front of several large baskets of food and blessing them before giving them to the hungry people. "My precious child, be generous in all you do and I will reward you a hundred fold. Give to those who are in need of food, clothing and shelter. These are the basic necessities of every human being. You cannot outdone in your generosity. I will multiply everything when you give in my name. Even with five loaves and two fish I was able to feed five thousand men. So give generously to the poor and I will bless you abundantly."

Lord Jesus, give me a generous heart especially toward the poor and the needy. May you be glorified and praised forever.

REFLECTION: Am I generous in giving my time and my resources to help other people who are less fortunate than I am?

SANCTIFY CHRIST

*"Sanctify Christ as Lord in your heart. Always
be ready to give an explanation to anyone
who asks you for a reason for your hope."*

1 PETER 3:15

In my vision I saw Jesus sitting on the throne inside my
heart. "My beloved, when you sanctify me within your
heart I become your Lord and Savior. You will be filled
with love, peace and joy. Your whole life will be transformed. You will look and act like me. You will have
hope no matter the situation you are in. So invite me
to live in your heart. This way your heart and mine will
beat as one. You will see and feel the world through my
eyes. You will be able to do great things because of me.
Let nothing separate us. Be united with me and you will
be filled with hope."

*Loving Jesus, you are my Lord and my
God. Please come and dwell in my heart.
Let me never be separated away from
you. For you are my hope and my joy.*

REFLECTION: Am I ready to give an explanation to
anyone who asks me for a reason for my hope?

I FORMED YOU

*"I formed you, and set you as a covenant
of the people, a light for the nations."*

ISAIAH 42:6

In my vision I saw a pregnant woman. "My child, I have formed you in your mother's womb. Your eyes, hands and feet are all according to my specifications. You are wonderfully made in my image and likeness. I have created you for a purpose. You are chosen and called to be my light for others. You have a mission and a destination in this world. Let not one day go by without fulfilling your call. Be vigilant, be courageous and be ready to serve others as I have done while I was in this world. Every day is a gift from God. Go forth and be my light and hope for others."

*Thank you, Jesus, for giving me life.
Yes, I will go and be your light of hope
for everyone I meet each day.*

REFLECTION: Am I willing to be a light for others as Jesus has chosen me to be?

BELIEVE

"Believe in the Lord Jesus and you and
your household will be saved."

ACTS 16:31

In my vision I saw Jesus laying hands upon each person who believed in him. "My beloved, it is true when you believe in me you and your household will be saved. The first step is for you to surrender yourself to me and you will see miracles abound. When you give your life to me, I can do great things through you. Believe in me and let my love spread to everyone around you. Let them see how blessed and joyful you are when you live according to my commandments. Trust in me with all your heart and let my light shine through you and to all your loved ones."

Lord Jesus, I believe in you. You are my
King of kings and Lord of lords. Help
me to increase my faith in you.

REFLECTION: Have I surrendered myself entirely to Jesus so that my household will be saved?

RIGHT THING TO DO

*"So for one who knows the right thing
to do and does not do it, it is a sin."*

JAMES 4:17

In my vision Jesus was sending out his disciples to each town to preach the gospel. "My faithful servant, you too are called to go and share the good news with others. This is the right thing for you to do no matter where you are. Your job is to spread my good news to everyone who is interested to hear my story. Do not be afraid nor be concerned on what to say. I will give you the right words to speak to them. My words will change their stony hearts into hearts of flesh. My words are full of wisdom and truth. Go and bring hope and joy to all you meet each day. Your reward will be great."

*Yes, my loving Jesus, I will go and proclaim all
that you have done for me. I will share your
story with those who are willing to listen.*

REFLECTION: Do I know that it is a sin not to share about Jesus and the truth with others?

I AM THE RESURRECTION

"I am the resurrection and the life; whoever
believes in me, even if he dies, will live."

JOHN 11:25

In my vision I saw Jesus talking to Martha as they
approached Lazarus' tomb. "My child, whoever believes
in me will live forever. Death cannot separate us. You are
mine. I have redeemed you on the cross from all your
sins and washed them clean by my blood and water. You
are set free. You will not perish but live with me for eternity. You are saved. You have nothing to fear. I will never
abandon you. I will always be there for you especially
when you need me most. Live each day in my arms and
you will have assurance that even when you die, you will
live forever with me in heaven."

Jesus, you are the resurrection and the life.
Thank you for saving me on the cross. You
have given me hope and abundant life.

REFLECTION: Do I believe that even when I die I
will live forever with Jesus in heaven?

YOUR JOY

"I will see you again, and your heart will rejoice,
and no one will take your joy away from you."

JOHN 16:22

In my vision I saw two lovers running towards each other's arms. "My love, soon I will be back and we will be united again. Do not be sad but be joyful knowing that this separation is only temporary. You know that I must go through the crucifixion before I can come back in my glorified body. Soon you will join me and enter into my kingdom in heaven. When that day comes your joy will be complete. You will have no more tears nor sorrow, but pure joy in union with me at my Father's house. So be glad and know that there is hope and a future waiting for you. Let your heart sing with joy."

My precious Jesus, you are my savior
and redeemer. I love you with all my
heart. You are the joy of my life.

REFLECTION: Do I look forward with joy when to being united with Jesus for eternity?

PRAYER OF FAITH

*"The prayer of faith will save the sick
person, and the Lord will raise him up."*

JAMES 5:15

In my vision I saw Peter praying over a sick child in bed and she was healed. "My beloved, you too are called to pray with the sick and to lay hands on them. Pray with expectant faith. Pray fervently and never give up. Every prayer of petition will be like an incense rising to my Father's throne room. He hears all your prayers, especially when you pray in my name for the sick and the needy. For my name has power to heal and to raise the dead. So do not be afraid to speak my words and quote the scripture. Never give up hope. Trust in my healing power."

*Thank you, Jesus, for your words of wisdom.
I will go and pray with those who need my
prayers. Fill me with your healing power.*

REFLECTION: Do I believe that Jesus has the power to heal the sick when I pray fervently for them?

WEALTH

*"How hard it is for those who have wealth
to enter the Kingdom of God!"*

MARK 10:23

In my vision I saw a man living in a large mansion. He was sitting at his desk busy counting his money. "My child, the rich people think that they do not need me in their daily life. They are self-sufficient. They have a beautiful home and lots of money to spend. But true happiness is not found in your wealth but in your relationship with me. Many wealthy people do not have time to spend with me. They are too busy making money. At the end of their lives they felt empty and unhappy. So my loving child, put me first in your life and everything else will be given to you. With me you will have more than you need."

*Loving Jesus, you are my wealth and my treasure.
You alone are my rock and my joy. With you I
will be able to enter your Kingdom one day.*

REFLECTION: Is Jesus the center of my life and everything else is secondary?

BE HOLY

"Be holy yourselves in every aspect
of your conduct, for it is written,
'Be holy because I am holy.'"

1 PETER 1:15-16

In vision I saw a father on the lookout for his son's return. "My little one, holiness is when you love others as I love you. Holiness is to forgive others and always be ready to do good to others. To be holy you need to live each day loving others especially those who are not lovable because they have never been loved. They will only learn how to love through you. By your love they will change their stony heart to a heart of flesh. Those who have been hurt are afraid to open their hearts. Perfect love cast out all fear. So be gentle and kind to all those who need my love. Be holy as I am holy."

Purify and cleanse my heart, Lord. Fill me
with more of your love so that I will be able
to love others as you have loved me.

REFLECTION: Do I try to be holy and love others as Jesus loves me?

TO SERVE

"For the Son of Man did not come to be served but to serve and to give his life as a ransom for many."

MARK 10:45

In my vision Jesus was washing his disciple's feet. "My faithful one, it is a joy to be able to serve others. When I was kneeling down to wash my disciples' feet, they realized how much I really love them. When you serve others, you are serving me. You will be changed and become more loving and caring. You will not regret it, because each time you lower yourself to serve others you are reaping rewards in heaven. Nothing you do for others will be in vain. Even the smallest kindness will not be forgotten. So remember to serve one another as I have served you and your joy will be complete."

My precious Jesus, thank you for teaching me how to serve others. I feel so blessed to be able to help others when they are in need.

REFLECTION: Do I go out of my way to serve others and treat them with love and kindness?

SING JOYFULLY

*"He will rejoice over you with gladness, and
renew you in his love. He will sing joyfully
because of you, as one sings at festivals."*

ZEPHANIAH 3:17-18

In my vision I saw Jesus singing and dancing at a wedding feast. "My loving child, be joyful and celebrate each day. Let your heart not be troubled. For I am with you and will take you to heaven one day to enjoy the wedding feast where there will be singing and dancing. You are my beloved child and I rejoice over you. I love you with an everlasting love. I will always cherish you. Live each day with joy in your heart. Let your mouth be filled with praises and thanksgiving. Rejoice and be glad for my Father loves you as much as I love you."

*Loving Jesus, you are the joy of my life. I want
to sing praises to you forever. I can hardly
wait for the day when I will see you face to
face and enjoy the banquet with you.*

REFLECTION: Do I wake up every morning feeling joyful and singing praises and thanksgiving to my loving God?

JUNE

BE HOSPITABLE

"Be hospitable to one another without complaining. As each one has received a gift, use it to serve one another as good stewards of God's varied grace."

In my vision I saw Mother Theresa caring for a dying person. "My precious one, every time when you help another person you are doing it to me. Because I love everyone. It is a joy to see my children loving and caring for each other. Be hospitable to everyone. Many people are lonely and have no friends. Some are sick and need your prayers. Some need advice and a good listening ear. Open your arms to all those who are hurting and lonely. Mother Theresa is a perfect model for you to follow. She is willing to help anyone who is in need. Do likewise and you will be rewarded greatly."

Lord, give me a generous heart and help me to go out of my way to help others. I want to love others as you have loved me.

REFLECTION: Am I hospitable to those who are lonely and neglected, and ready to welcome them?

PERSEVERE

"If we died with him we shall also live with him;
if we persevere we shall also reign with him."

2 TIMOTHY 2:11-12

In my vision I saw a person rock climbing. He was harnessed to the rock and to his partner. After much effort he finally reached the top of the mountain and he stood there enjoying the beautiful view from above. "My loving child, so it is with your life. When you are harnessed with me and to the commandments, you will reach your goal safely. Every effort and perseverance you make will bring you closer to my Kingdom in heaven. Do not give up! Continue to persevere with all your strength. I will be there to guide you and to protect you from falling. You will reach your destination."

My Jesus, you are my rock and my salvation.
Help me to persevere till the end. I want
to be with you in heaven one day.

REFLECTION: Do I ask Jesus to help me persevere till the end, especially when I am too weak to go on alone?

FEED MY SHEEP

"'Lord, you know everything, you know that I love you.' Jesus said to him, 'Feed my sheep.'"

JOHN 21:17

In my vision I saw a little child throwing pieces of bread to feed the birds around him. "Yes, my little one, you are that child in your vision. Give my bread and my body to all that come around you. Feed them with my words and let them know how much I love them. Because each person is precious to me. I want to fill them with my Holy Spirit, my joy, my love and my hope. Go and spread my word around to everyone who is open to receive me. Go and feed them with my blessings. Encourage them to come to me and their lives will never be the same again."

Your words are my daily bread, O lord. I will feed your words to everyone who has ears to hear and heart to receive them.

REFLECTION: Have I told others about Jesus, especially those who are hungry to know more about him?

VIRTUE

> *"Make every effort to supplement your faith*
> *with virtue, virtue with knowledge, knowledge*
> *with self-control, self-control with endurance,*
> *endurance with devotion, devotion with*
> *mutual affection, mutual affection with love."*
>
> 2 PETER 1:5-7

In my vision I saw Mary cooking and washing dishes in her little kitchen. "My child, my mother Mary is a perfect example of a woman with virtue. She had all the qualities of a virtuous person. She carried me in her womb for nine months and cared for my needs for 30 years. When I was thirteen, she searched for me for three days until she finally found me in the temple. She stood at the foot of the cross until I took my last breath. Mary loved everyone. Her arms were always open ready to show affection and mercy. Pray for more virtue daily and one day you too will be as loving as my mother Mary."

> *Jesus, I want to imitate your mother*
> *Mary and learn from her how to be a*
> *virtuous person. Teach me to love you*
> *and others more and more each day.*

REFLECTION: Do I live a virtuous life like Mary, always sacrificing and surrendering myself to Jesus' will?

ETERNAL LIFE

> *"Now this is eternal life, that they should*
> *know you, the only true God, and one*
> *whom you sent, Jesus Christ."*
>
> JOHN 17:3

In my vision I saw Jesus rowing a boat with people sitting close to him. "My beloved child, anyone who is with me will have eternal life. For I will lead you to my Father's house where there will be no more tears and sorrow. Where I am, you will also be. I have saved you from this sinful world. As long as you are journeying with me, you will not be lost but will have abundant life. No evil one will be able to harm you. Stay close to me and never wander off on your own. I am your Savior and your redeemer. If you believe in me you will be saved."

> *Lord Jesus, thank you for saving me from*
> *eternal damnation. I believe you are the savior*
> *of the world. I praise you and I adore you.*

REFLECTION: Am I in the same boat with Jesus so that one day I will spend eternal life with him?

LIKE THE ANGELS

*"When they rise from the dead, they
neither marry nor are given in marriage,
but they are like the angels in heaven."*

MARK 12:25

In my vision I saw legions of angels surrounding the throne where God the Father was seated. "My precious one, you too have a guardian angel surrounding you always. When you die you will be like the angels filled with love and light. You will have a new body and will live forever with me in heaven where there is no more sorrow but only love and joy. You will be surrounded by angels who will be ministering to you. Your eyes will be opened and you will see all those who have gone before you. So be patient and wait. That day will soon come and the angels will lead you to heaven."

*Loving Jesus, I long for the day when I will be
united with you in heaven and see you face to face.*

REFLECTION: Can I imagine that when I die one day I will be like the angel in heaven?

KEEP ME SAFE

"Keep me safe, O God; in you I take refuge."
PSALM 16:1

In my vision I saw myself dressed in the armor of God. I had a helmet on my head and a breastplate with a belt while holding a sword in one hand and a shield on the other. "My beloved, I am your shield and your armor. Put on Christ and you will be safe. Remember to call on me when you need me. I am your protector and your savior. Rely on me not on human beings. Those who trust in me will not perish. Everyone who is given to me by my Father will be safe. For nothing will happen to you without my Father's consent. His will for you is always good. So trust in me completely."

Lord Jesus, you are my refuge and protector from all my enemies. Never let me be separated from you. I trust you with my whole heart.

REFLECTION: Do I put on the armor of God every morning when I get dressed?

DO NOT WEEP

"When the Lord saw her, he was moved with pity for her and said to her, 'Do not weep.'"

LUKE 7:13

In my vision Jesus was wiping the tears of a widow who had just lost her only son. "My loving child, do not give up hope. For I am the resurrection and the life. Whoever believes in me will have everlasting life. Even though things might seem hopeless, all I have to do is to say the word and everything will be changed. Like the widow's son who came alive when I told the boy to arise. There was such rejoicing. So always remember to come to me with all your problems. Put them in my hands and I can transform your weeping into joy. I can make all things new."

My Lord and my God! I do believe that you can change my weeping into joy. Remind me to always turn to you when I am in sorrow.

REFLECTION: Do I go to Jesus whenever I am sad or feel hopeless and helpless?

ANGRY

> *"Whoever is angry with his brother*
> *will be liable to judgement."*
> MATTHEW 5:22

In my vision I saw two people fighting in the street. "My child, it breaks my heart to see when two of my beloved children are angry with each other. It is my hope that everyone can live in peace and love with one another. Anger and hatred is not from God but from the evil one who is trying to destroy what I have created you to be. Do not be angry with anyone but learn to forgive and to be humble. Humility is never proud. Humility is merciful and kind to others. Love is patient and slow to anger. Love is eager to go out of one's way to help another. Forgive others and you will be forgiven."

> *Merciful Jesus, please forgive me for all the times when I was angry with others. Give me more of your love and kindness. Help me to hold my tongue when I am angry.*

REFLECTION: Do I have anger and hatred for anyone in my heart?

FORGIVEN

"Amen, I say to you, all sins and all blasphemies
that people utter will be forgiven them."

MARK 3:28

In my vision I saw a prodigal son returning home to his father's house. "My love, people think that there are serious sins that cannot be forgiven. I tell you when you come to me and ask for forgiveness I will always forgive you. The only sin that cannot be forgiven is when you do not believe in my infinite mercy and power to forgive. Many people cannot forgive themselves and think that I too will not forgive them. That is a lie! I will forgive your sin as long as you repent and ask for forgiveness. So never hesitate to confess your sins. I will always welcome you back with my open arms."

Thank you, Jesus, for forgiving all my past sins.
Keep me pure and deliver me from the evil one.

REFLECTION: Do I believe that Jesus will always forgive and welcome me back no matter how serious my sin is?

PEACEMAKERS

*"Blessed are the peacemakers, for they
will be called children of God."*

MATTHEW 5:9

In my vision I saw two men shaking hands and a dove hovering above them. "My precious one, every time you help people to seek peace instead of war you are acting as my beloved child. I love all human beings because they are created in my Father's image and likeness. It pains me to see when people are killing each other. I created each one of you with flesh and blood, and a heart to love. When people turn to hate and anger, they are not acting as my children. For my children are those who forgive and make peace. You are my child. Come and imitate me to be a peacemaker for everyone around you."

*My beloved Jesus, help me to be your
peacemaker everywhere I go. Let there
be peace in this troubled world.*

REFLECTION: Am I acting like a child of God and bringing peace to everyone?

ENCOURAGE ONE ANOTHER

"Mend your ways, encourage one another, agree with one another, live in peace, and the God of love and peace will be with you."

2 CORINTHIANS 13:11

In my vision I saw a toddler walking towards his mother who was encouraging him every step he took. "My child, be an encourager to one another, like the mother in your vision who never scolded her child but helped him to get up every time he fell. So it is with you. I have watched you and helped you to grow each day in your walk towards me. I have never failed to uphold and encourage you with my loving words. Do likewise to those who are trying to grow spiritually. They need to be encouraged and coached with tender love and assurance. Be with them as they journey towards me."

O loving Jesus, thank you for all the times you have encouraged and guided me. Teach me to do the same to others.

REFLECTION: Have I encouraged others with loving words as they journey towards Jesus?

BLOOD AND WATER

*"One soldier thrust his lance into his side, and
immediately blood and water flowed out."*

JOHN 19:34

In my vision I saw an image of Divine Mercy Jesus standing with rays of red and white flooding out of his heart. "My beloved, you have no idea how much I have suffered for you because of my love for you. I was scourged at the pillar, crowned with thorns and nailed on the cross so that all your sins are forgiven. I have washed you clean with my living water and filled your heart with my precious blood. Go forth now and love others the same way as I have loved you. Have mercy and compassion for everyone as I have showered upon you."

*Merciful and loving Jesus, thank you for all
you have suffered for my sins. Make my heart
as compassionate and loving as yours.*

REFLECTION: Do I realize how much Jesus has suffered for the love of me?

GIVE

> *"Give to the one who asks of you, and do not turn your back on one who wants to borrow."*
>
> MATTHEW 5:42

In my vision I saw a beggar asking for alms. "My child, never send anyone away empty handed. Give and share whatever you have with others. Be generous as I have been generous with you. The more you give to others, the more my Father will bless you. Give not from your head but from your heart. Let your mercy extend to everyone. This way, when you are in need, others will also give to you generously. You reap what you sow. Be ready to give to others more than what they are asking from you. Only in this way you will convert souls. They will see me in you and know how much I love them."

Yes, Lord, I will go and give to everyone who asks from me. Give me a generous heart so that you may be glorified through me.

REFLECTION: Am I generous and always ready to share what I have with others?

RIGHTEOUSNESS

> *"Unless your righteousness surpasses that of the scribes and Pharisees, you will not enter into the kingdom of heaven."*
>
> MATTHEW 5:20

In my vision Jesus was teaching his disciples. "My faithful one, only those who are humble and obedient will enter into the kingdom of heaven. Remember that I have chosen ordinary people to be my disciples. Peter, James and John were all fishermen. They were humble and uneducated men and yet they had great love and obedience to my teaching. They did what I have told them to do. They believed in me and were willing to lay down their lives for me in order to spread my good news to the ends of the world. You too are called to be righteous if you obey and do what I commanded you to do."

Thank you, Lord Jesus, for your words of wisdom and encouragement. I want to be righteous in your sight.

REFLECTION: Am I a righteous and humble person in the eyes of Jesus?

OFFER NO RESISTANCE

"Offer no resistance to one who is evil.
When someone strikes you on your right
cheek, turn the other one to him as well."

MATTHEW 5:39

In my vision I saw Jesus being slapped and spit upon by the soldiers around him. "My child, let every action you do be loving and kind. Even when people insult you or hurt you. Do not retaliate nor fight back. For I am with you. Your enemies will not triumph over you but will regret their actions at the end. If you want to imitate me, then you need to offer no resistance when people ill treat you. For the revenge is mine. I will make sure that those who are faithful to my teaching will not perish but will live forever. Be a model for others to follow."

Lord Jesus, it is not easy to let others to
ill treat me. Help me to love all those who
do not love me, especially my enemies.

REFLECTION: Do I retaliate or fight back when people ill treat me?

LIFE OF JESUS

*"For we who live are constantly being given up
to death for the sake of Jesus, so that the life of
Jesus may be manifested in our mortal flesh."*

In my vision I saw people pushing wheel chaired people to a church for healing. "My beloved, every time you bring others to me you are living my life as I would have done. I have no hands and feet now except yours. So, when you sacrifice your time to go out and bring others to me, you are living as I would when I was in this world. I have compassion for all the poor and the sick because they are so helpless. They need me and yet they cannot come to me without your help. My faithful servant, let me live in you daily. Only in this way you will carry out my mission. Thank you for doing my will."

*O loving and caring Jesus, I am willing to lay
down my life for you. Show me how to be your
instrument in everything I do each day.*

REFLECTION: Am I willing to sacrifice myself and help those who are less fortunate than I am -- as Jesus did?

YES

"Let your 'Yes' mean 'Yes,' and your 'No' mean 'No.' Anything more is from the evil one."

In my vision I saw Mary went in haste to visit her cousin Elizabeth and to help her. "My love, when you hear me calling you to do a job, let your "Yes" be like Mary who went in haste to help her cousin Elizabeth during her pregnancy. Her actions spoke louder than words. Imitate her and do not be afraid but have complete confidence in me. I will send angels to guide you and to protect you. You need not fear nor worry. Everything will go well. All you need is to step out of your comfort zone and say "Yes". You will be rewarded greatly for your obedience to my call."

Yes, my dearest Jesus, I will follow you wherever you send me. Give me the courage and the strength to do your will.

REFLECTION: Have I changed my mind after I have said "Yes" to someone and broken my promise?

JUDGEMENT SEAT

"For we must all appear before the judgement seat of Christ, so that each may receive recompense, according to what he did in the body, whether good or evil."

2 CORINTHIANS 5:10

In my vision I saw myself standing in front of the throne room ready to be judged. "My child, every person will be judged for all the things that he has done or failed to do. You too will be judged one day. But I will be standing beside you and helping you to remember all the times when you were obedient and followed my commandments. I will give you the courage to face the truth. You will see your whole life flash in front of you. Do not despair. There is still time to do good for me. It is never too late. Let today be the beginning of a new chapter and try to live each day for the honor and glory of God."

Thank you, Lord Jesus, for helping me to start each day anew. Let me be more loving and caring from today on.

REFLECTION: Am I prepared to be judged by Jesus for everything I have done in my entire life?

TREASURES ON EARTH

> *"Do not store up for yourselves treasures on earth, where moth and decay destroy, and thieves break in and steal."*
>
> MATTHEW 6:19

In my vision I saw a rich man counting his money. Suddenly there was a big fire and all his money were burned. "My beloved, earthly treasures do not last long. They will all perish and will bring you grief. When you store up treasures in heaven they will last forever. What are the treasures in heaven? It is your love for God and for your neighbor. These two will never perish. For love is eternal. Love can move mountains and change people's hearts. Love is the ultimate treasure. Seek God first and you will be able to love everyone around you. And you will be rewarded greatly in heaven."

Yes, Jesus, I will love God and others as you have loved me. Help me to seek you above everything else, for you are my treasure.

REFLECTION: Is Jesus my most precious treasure in this world? Do I love him above everyone else?

LIVING BREAD

*"I am the living bread that came down from
heaven; whoever eats this bread will live forever."*

JOHN 6:51

In my vision I saw a host with a red heart pulsating and
glowing with radiant light. "My love, every time when
you receive communion, you are receiving my heart
which is alive and will give you life. For I am the way, the
truth and the LIFE. With me, you will have abundant
life, a life full of love and joy. Come to the Eucharist as
often as you can. I am always ready to be united with
you, one heart and one mind. I will transform your
heart into my heart. When people see you, they will see
my love radiating from your heart. I am the bread of
life; whoever eats my body and drinks my blood will live
forever."

*Thank you, Jesus, for giving me your
precious body and blood to eat and drink.
Nourish and strengthen me every time
when I receive you into my heart.*

REFLECTION: Do I truly believe that if I receive the
body and the blood of Jesus I will live forever?

DAY OF SALVATION

*"Behold, now is a very acceptable time;
behold now is the day of salvation."*

2 CORINTHIANS 6:2

In my vision Jesus was walking by the sea and when he saw James and John mending their nets, he told them to follow him. "My faithful one, now is the time to drop whatever you have on your own agenda and come to follow me. When you leave behind your own plans, you are free to do my will. Do not look back to your old way of living but follow me wherever I am leading you. Your life will never be the same again. You will be able to do great things that seemed impossible for you. But with me all things are possible. Are you ready to follow me and walk in my way of salvation?"

*My Jesus and my Savior, I will follow
you wherever you want me to go. Never
let me be separated away from you.*

REFLECTION: Am I ready to leave behind my own will and follow Jesus wherever he leads me?

DO NOT WORRY

> *"Do not worry about tomorrow;*
> *tomorrow will take care of itself.*
> *Sufficient for a day is its own evil."*
>
> MATTHEW 6:34

In my vision I saw a father carrying his child on his shoulders and holding his little hands. The child was laughing and giggling with pleasure. "My precious, you are my delight. Learn to laugh and enjoy each moment of your life. Let nothing worry you. For you are in the palm of my hands. I will hold you and be with you always. No evil one can snatch you away from me. You are mine. Be like the little child in your vision. Be happy and content. Trust in me with all your heart. Do not worry about what to eat or drink. You know that you will never lack of anything. I will provide for all your needs."

> *Loving Jesus, I know that you will provide*
> *all my needs and my deepest desires. I want*
> *to trust you more and more each day.*

REFLECTION: Do I worry about what I am going to eat or wear each day?

WOODEN BEAM

> *"You hypocrite, remove the wooden beam
> from your eye first; then you will see clearly to
> remove the splinter from your brother's eye."*
>
> MATTHEW 7:5

In my vision I saw a person pointing a finger at another. "My child, remember when you judge another person, three more fingers will be pointing back to you. In this world no one is perfect. Everyone has faults. Try to work on your own weaknesses before pointing out the faults of others. It is far more effective if you praise and encourage one another than fault finding. When people are humiliated they will not appreciate what you have said to them even if it is the truth. Never give corrections unless they ask for your advice. Treat others as you would like them to treat you."

> *Jesus, you are all wise and perfect. Help me
> to see my own wooden beam before trying
> to remove another person's splinter.*

REFLECTION: Do I judge and criticize others instead of giving them words of encouragement?

INNER ROOM

> *"When you pray, go to your inner room, close the door, and pray to your Father in secret. And your Father who sees in secret will repay you."*
>
> MATTHEW 6:6

In my vision I saw myself kneeling down by my bed and praying. "My beloved, every time when you pray from your heart I hear you. I love you and I care about you. Your heartfelt prayer goes straight to my Father's throne room. We know all your needs and your prayers will always be answered. Sometimes your wishes may be delayed because my timing is better than yours. I know the future and all the circumstances. So place all your trust in me. I hear you and understand what you are going through. If you only knew the power of your prayer you would pray constantly without ceasing."

Lord Jesus, thank you for always hearing my prayers even when I pray in secret. You are my hiding place and my fortress.

REFLECTION: How often do I go to my inner room and pray to Jesus from my heart?

PEARLS BEFORE SWINE

> *"Do not give what is holy to dogs, or throw your pearls before swine, lest they trample them underfoot, and turn and tear you to pieces."*
>
> MATTHEW 7:6

In my vision I saw a man throwing a juicy steak to a vicious dog. As soon as it ate the meat the dog quickly attacked the person for more. "My child, do not argue or give the pearls of wisdom to those who are not willing to accept them. They will only make fun of you and tear you into pieces. Their minds are made up. Instead of receiving your good intentions they will look down upon you with scorn. Because they do not want to change their way of living. They think that they are smarter than you. Pray for them and forgive them for they know not what they are doing."

Lord Jesus, give me the wisdom and the discernment on how to deal with those who are not ready to hear the good news about you.

REFLECTION: Do I pray for those who are not ready to receive the truth about Jesus?

BEAR GOOD FRUIT

*"Every good tree bears good fruit, and
a rotten tree bears bad fruit."*

MATTHEW 7:17

In my vision I saw a beautiful green tree with pears hanging from its branches. "My beloved, you are called to do good deeds for others. Those who do not produce good fruit are selfish and self-centered. They never think about other people's needs. They are only concerned about themselves. Imitate me. I came into this world to lay down my life for you. There is nothing I would not do for your salvation. So you too must do the same for others. If you love me, you will want to follow my example. Go and bear good fruit so that my Kingdom will come."

*My loving Jesus, help me to do at least one
good deed each day. I want to bear good
fruit for your honor and glory, Lord.*

REFLECTION: Am I concerned about other people's needs and gone out of my way to help them?

HOUSE ON THE ROCK

"Everyone who listens to these words of mine and acts on them will be like a wise man who built his house on rock."

MATTHEW 7:24

In my vision I saw a house built on stilts. When a storm came the stilts gave way and the house fell. "My faithful one, some people who pick and choose my commandments and my words are like a house built on stilts. They will not survive when persecution comes. But you, my loving child, have listened to my words and kept my statutes. Your house is built on my rock. You will be able to stand and survive through all trials. You will not fall. Put all your trust on me and my words of wisdom. Study the scripture day and night. Only in this way you will be saved."

Jesus, you are my rock and my salvation. Give me the wisdom to always listen to your voice and follow your commandments.

REFLECTION: Do I follow all the commandments that God has given me and trust in his words of wisdom?

RESCUE ME

> *"The Lord will rescue me from every evil threat and will bring me safe to his heavenly kingdom."*
>
> 2 TIMOTHY 4:18

In my vision I saw myself almost accidently falling off a cliff. But Jesus was right there holding on to my right arm and bringing me back to safety. "My precious child, hold on to me and you will never perish. I will keep you safe in my loving arms. You can count on me. Place your trust upon no one except me. For human beings will fail you, but I will never forsake you. You are my treasure and my delight. I will hold you in my arms like a mother holding her baby. You can rest and feel secure. Have peace in your heart and know that I am always with you."

> *Most loving Jesus, you are always ready to rescue me from the evil one and protect me from all harm. Thank you, Jesus.*

REFLECTION: Do I trust Jesus whole heartily instead of other human beings in my life?

BORE OUR DISEASES

*"He took away our infirmities
and bore our diseases."*

<small>MATTHEW 8:17</small>

In my vision I saw Jesus suffering with pain as the soldiers were nailing him to the cross. "My child, I have suffered tremendously on the cross so that you might have life. I have carried your sins and illnesses with me to the cross. You are healed and set free. Claim it! Believe in it. Live each day with joy and thanksgiving. Have faith in me and live an abundant life. By my stripes you are healed. See how none of my disciples were burdened with illness or disease. They were invigorated every time that they carried out my mission. They rejoiced even when they were chained and beaten. Do likewise."

*Heal me, O Lord, that I may be healed
so that I will be able to go out and to
proclaim all that you have done for me.*

REFLECTION: Do I believe that I can be healed and set free by his wounds and suffering for me on the cross?

JULY

I DESIRE MERCY

> *"Go and learn the meaning of the words, I desire mercy, not sacrifice."*
> MATTHEW 9:13

In my vision I saw Jesus' loving heart radiating with light. "My beloved, have mercy upon everyone around you. Do not think yourself better than others that just because you have not murdered or committed adultery that you are better than them. No one is perfect except my Father in heaven. Everyone has sinned. So learn to love everyone with mercy and compassion. If you were born in similar circumstances you might act the same way as they did. Everyone needs love and mercy. See how I lavish my love upon those who need me most. Go and do the same and you will be rewarded greatly."

> *Loving and merciful Jesus, teach me to be more and more like you in everything I do each day. Give me a merciful and compassionate heart.*

REFLECTION: Do I show love and mercy towards everyone around me?

SEEK GOOD

> *"Seek good and not evil, that you may*
> *live; then truly will the Lord, the God*
> *of hosts, be with you as you claim."*
>
> AMOS 5:14

In my vision I saw a person with a flashlight looking for something in the dark. "My child, invite me to be with you every day. Do not wonder off into darkness alone. With me you will see everything more clearly. For I will shine my light upon the right way you need to go. Without me you will be easily lost in this evil world. With me by your side you will see goodness everywhere you go. You will not be tempted nor stumble and fall. I am the Light of the World. If you follow me closely, I will lead you into the right path."

> *Lord Jesus, help me to seek good and to avoid*
> *evil everywhere I go. Shine your light upon me*
> *so that I will not be lost in this evil world.*

REFLECTION: Do I have the light of Christ in my heart so that I can see goodness everywhere I go?

REJOICING

> *"The seventy-two returned rejoicing, and said, 'Lord, even the demons are subject to us because of your name.'"*
>
> LUKE 10:17

In my vision I saw a large group of people with their hands raised, rejoicing and praising God. "My dear child, when you praise my name you will feel joyful. Every time when you step out to do my will your heart will rejoice, because whatever you ask of me I will give it to you. Doors will be opened and walls will crumble when you work for me. I will lead your way and the evil one will fall as lightning. They will run before your eyes. Where I am, the evil one will flee. Only legions of angels will be there. Seeing my light shining through you all the demons will scatter. So rejoice and be glad!"

> *All praise and glory be yours, my King and my Savior, Lord Jesus Christ. Thank you for your mighty name.*

REFLECTION: When I call on the name of Jesus do I believe that the demons will flee?

HEART'S DESIRE

*"If you find your delight in the Lord,
he will grant your heart's desire."*

PSALM 37:4

In my vision I saw a priest praying in front of the crucifix totally engrossed in his ecstasy. "My precious one, when you are truly in love with me how can I refuse you when you ask me for anything? I will always grant your wishes whenever you ask from me. So delight in me with all your heart and I will grant every wish of your heart's desires. You can count on me. I will never disappoint you. Whatever you ask of me it will be done. For you are my delight. Love and treasure me above all else and your reward will be great beyond your expectations."

My Lord and my delight, you alone I love and treasure. Thank you for answering all my prayers.

REFLECTION: Do I believe that Jesus delights in me and will grant all my heart's desires?

I WILL ESPOUSE YOU

> *"I will espouse you to me forever; I will espouse you in right and in justice, in love and in mercy."*
>
> HOSEA 3:21

In my vision I saw Jesus putting a gold ring on my index finger. I was overjoyed. "My beloved, I long to hold you in my arms. You are precious to me. You cannot imagine how much I love you. I laid down my life for you so that you are set free. Free to be my spouse. Free to come into my Kingdom without a blemish. You are mine and we belong to each other. There is no one in this world who can replace you. You are unique and wonderfully made. I love you with an everlasting love. My deepest desire is for you to spend eternity with me in heaven. Come to the wedding feast."

> *O Jesus, my love, I adore you and I love you.*
> *I am all yours. Take me and hold me tight.*
> *Never let me be separated away from you.*

REFLECTION: Is it my deepest desire to spend eternity united with Jesus in heaven?

PEACE TO YOU

> *"He came and preached peace to you who were far off and peace to those who were near."*
>
> EPHESIANS 2:17

In my vision I saw people singing together, "Let there be peace on earth and let it begin with me..." "My child, when you are in turmoil and stressed, come to me and I will give you my peace which is beyond your understanding. When you pray, visualize my presence and your heart will stop pounding. You will feel peace and calm again. For I am the Prince of Peace and King of kings. With me at your side you have nothing to worry about. Even though everything around you might crumble, you will be saved. Come, my precious one, and receive my peace into your heart."

> *Thank you, Lord Jesus, for your assurance.*
> *I feel peaceful whenever I am with you.*
> *You are my rock and my savior.*

REFLECTION: Is Jesus my Prince of peace and King of kings?

TWELVE DISCIPLES

*"Jesus summoned his twelve disciples and gave
them authority over unclean spirits to drive them
out and to cure every disease and every illness."*

MATTHEW 10:1

In my vision I saw Peter and John talking to a lame beggar who was healed. He was jumping, leaping and praising God. "My beloved, you too are given the authority to drive out demons and to cure the sick. Every disciple has the authority to do these things as long as you call on my name and believe in your heart that I am the healer and the redeemer for everyone for asks for healing. Be my hands and lay them on people who ask for healing and deliverance. I will do it. Have faith in me and know that I will be there for you and will grant you whatever you ask in my name."

*Merciful Jesus, you are truly our healer.
Thank you for calling me to be your disciple
and to witness so many miracles of healing
when I pray with the sick in your name.*

REFLECTION: Am I aware that Jesus is calling me to cast out the evil one and to cure the sick with his healing power?

I BLESS YOU

*"Every day will I bless you; I will praise
your name forever and ever."*

PSALM 145:2

In my vision I saw a woman holding a bowl of incense
in her hands and the smoke rising up unto the air. "My
loving child, every praise and thanksgiving that you
offer up to me are precious to me. They are like music to
my ears and incense rising straight into my heart. Not
one word will be lost in the smoke. Your prayers and
praises will go directly to heaven. Remember to praise
often throughout the day. Praise will lift your spirits and
refocus your attention on me instead of your daily problems. Praise will enlighten your mind and bring joy to
your heart."

*I praise you and I bless you, my Lord and
my God. You are my good Shephard and my
Savior. May you be blessed forever and ever.*

REFLECTION: How often do I praise and bless Jesus
for all that he has done for me?

ACKNOWLEDGE ME

*"Everyone who acknowledges me before others I
will acknowledge before my heavenly Father."*

Matthew 10:32

In my vision Jesus was standing next to me introducing
me to his heavenly Father. "My child, every time when
you acknowledge me to all your friends and family I feel
really loved. I will do the same for you when you pass
from this life to the next. I will bring you to my heavenly
Father and introduce you to Him and to all my brothers and sisters in heaven. There will be great celebration
when that day comes. You will be loved by everyone
because of me. They will welcome you with open arms.
So remember to always acknowledge me to others. Let
me be your best friend forever."

*Yes, my precious Jesus, I am proud to
have you as my best friend. I want all
my friends to know and to love you.*

REFLECTION: Do I acknowledge Jesus to my family,
friends and all the people around me?

SPIRIT OF CHRIST

*"Whoever does not have the Spirit of
Christ does not belong to him."*

<small>ROMANS 8:9</small>

In my vision I saw myself putting on Christ like the armor of God. "My beloved, on the day of your baptism my Spirit came into your soul. From that day on, my Spirit lives in you. Everything you do glorifies me and brings me honor. Be aware that I live in your heart. When you pray, I answer you. When you suffer, I suffer with you and when you dance with joy, I also leap with joy. We become one in the spirit. Do not forget that I am a central part of your being. Nothing can separate my love for you. When people see you, they will see my light shining through you. You belong to me, my dearest child."

*Lord Jesus Christ, it is so comforting to know
that you dwell in my heart. May I be one with
you as you are with your heavenly Father.*

REFLECTION: Do I realize that when I was baptized, the Spirit of Christ came into my soul?

REBELLIOUS HOUSE

"They have eyes to see but do not see,
and ears to hear but do not hear, for
they are such a rebellious house!"

EZEKIEL 12:2

In my vision a saw a crowd of people protesting and shouting on the street. "My child, do not go with the crowd. For they have forgotten me. They are always grumbling and discontent with everything. They only know how to complain and forgot that I am the solution to every problem. They try to solve the world situation on their own which is a losing battle. Turn to me, my child, and I will show you the proper way to conquer all evil. Pray and turn your life around first and you will no longer be rebellious nor in despair. Keep your eyes open and focus on me alone. All will be well."

Jesus, you came into the world to save us. Let me
never forget that you are in charge of everything.
Open my eyes, Lord, that I may see you.

REFLECTION: Am I rebellious and always complaining and grumbling about everything?

MY STRENGTH

> *"My strength and my courage is the Lord, and he has been my salvation."*
>
> ISAIAH 12:2

In my vision I saw a lighthouse sitting on a solid rock. Even though there were storms ragging around it, the house stood there unharmed. "My precious one, I am your rock and your savior. As long as you stand with me you will have the strength and courage to overcome all sickness and tribulations. You will not be overcome. You are saved and will not perish but live for eternity with me in heaven. Let your light shine to all who are around you. Let them see your peace and joy. Stand firm on me. Rest assured that you will have the strength and the courage to overcome all circumstances."

> *You are my rock and my salvation, O Lord. In you alone will I trust. Please give me the strength and the courage to face each day with joy.*

REFLECTION: Do I believe that Jesus is my rock and he will help me overcome all trials and tribulations?

WE HAVE REDEMPTION

"In him we have redemption by his blood, the forgiveness of transgressions, in accord with the riches of his grace that he lavished upon us."

EPHESIANS 1:7-8

In my vision I saw Jesus dressed all in white rising into heaven with radiant light. "My beloved, I have suffered and died on the cross so that you can be redeemed. I have shed my precious blood for every sin that you have committed against my Father. By my grace you are set free and have inherited eternal life in heaven. I will lavish you with my love and mercy. You are mine. You belong to me and I will always treasure you in my heart. For I have paid a steep price for your redemption. One day you too will join me in heaven where there are no more tears nor sorrow."

Thank you, my most loving and merciful Jesus, for redeeming me from all my sins. Fill me with your grace.

REFLECTION: Is Jesus my savior and my redeemer?

KINDNESS AND TRUTH

"Kindness and truth shall meet;
justice and peace shall kiss."

PSALM 85:11

In my vision I saw Jesus teaching on the mountain to a crowd of people around him. "My children, be kind to one another and live in the truth always. This way you will have peace in your heart. Kindness covers all ill feelings that other people have against you and vice versa. Truth will set you free. When you live in the truth you will be able to sleep soundly every night, because you know that you are walking with me in the right path. Be kind and merciful to all, even those who persecute you. In this way they will see their own wrongdoing and they will change their hearts."

My beloved Jesus, help me to remember to
be kind and truthful to everyone. I want
to imitate you in everything I do.

REFLECTION: Have I been kind to others and tried to live in the truth?

WHOEVER ENDURES

> *"You will be hated by all because of my name, but whoever endures to the end will be saved."*
>
> MATTHEW 10:22

In my vision I saw a person with his hands and feet tied to a post being tortured. "My love, many martyrs suffered greatly because of me. They will not stop praising my name. They are true models for you to follow. When they suffer because of me, the people around them will realize how much they love me. True love is when one lays down one's life for another. That is the ultimate love and sacrifice. That is what I have suffered and endured for you and for your salvation. So be brave when you are persecuted. Endure to the end and your reward will be great in heaven."

> *Lord Jesus, thank you for suffering and dying on the cross for me. Give me the strength to endure suffering to the end for your honor and glory.*

REFLECTION: Do I ask Jesus to help me when I am persecuted and treated poorly by others?

SPARROWS

"Do not be afraid; you are worth more than many sparrows."

MATTHEW 10:31

In my vision I saw a little bird perched on a branch singing a beautiful toon. "My little one, you are more precious to me than any animal. You are made in my image and likeness. Fear not. I am with you always. Be content and be happy. Feel my loving arms around you at all times especially when you are afraid. You are the apple of my eye. Does a baby feel afraid when he is being held? No, he loves every moment of it. He feels so content and secure in his mother's arms. So do not worry about anything. Trust in me with all your heart and know that I will always be there for you."

Hold me tight and never let me go. With your arms around me I will not be afraid. My loving Jesus, you are my protector and my shelter.

REFLECTION: How much do I trust and have faith in Jesus' loving care for me in my daily life?

MY BURDEN LIGHT

"For my yoke is easy, and my burden light."
MATTHEW 11:30

In my vision I saw two cows yoked together and pulling a heavy cart on a rocky road. "My child, put your burdens upon me. Never try to carry your load alone. Put it on my shoulder and I will carry it with you. You need not suffer alone, but always remember to seek my assistance. With me at your side you will feel more confident. You will be able to go further than you thought. Alone, you will soon be burned out and grow weary. Take my yoke upon you and follow my footsteps. Never be too proud to ask for my help. Surrender yourself to me and I will carry your burden with you."

My Jesus, I can do nothing without you.
Remind me to be yoked with you in
everything I do for you each day.

REFLECTION: When I am burned out and feel burdened do I ask Jesus to help me to carry the load?

HE BRINGS JUSTICE

*"A bruised reed he will not break, a
smoldering wick he will not quench,
until he brings justice to victory."*

MATTHEW 12:20

In my vision I saw a hand holding a scale with weights
on it. "My beloved, I came into this world to deliver
everyone from corruption and sin. I want to show you
how to live a just and righteous life. I am the Way, the
Truth and the Life. When you follow me, you will keep
my commandments. For I am a merciful and compassionate God who will judge everyone justly. If you listen
to my word and keep it in your heart you will act lovingly towards all your brethren. You will try to imitate
me and bring justice everywhere you go. Remember you
will have victory at the end."

*Lord Jesus, you are the one who brought
justice into this world. Teach me to be
merciful and just to everyone.*

REFLECTION: Am I trying to live a just and righteous life imitating Jesus in every day of my life?

MY BROTHER

> *"Whoever does the will of my heavenly Father*
> *is my brother, and sister and mother."*
>
> MATTHEW 12:50

In my vision I saw Jesus calling me and leading me to meet his heavenly Father. "My precious one, whenever you do my Father's will, you are acting as a part of my family. You become my brother and sister. I will bring you closer to Him. When you say "yes" to my commandments you are acting as a child of God. From now on, you are protected and cherished as my own. All you need to do is to ask and trust that it shall be done for you. For my Father loves everyone who trusts me and loves me. Go forth and love one another as I have loved you."

> *Heavenly Father, to do your will is my delight.*
> *Jesus, you are my brother and my savior.*
> *It is so good to be a part of your family.*

REFLECTION: Do I live my life as a child of God and treating everyone as my brothers and sisters in the Lord?

THORNS

> "Some seed fell among thorns, and the
> thorns grew up and choked it."
>
> MATTHEW 13:7

In my vision I saw a thorny bush and nothing grows around it. "My child, you need to weed and water often. Because when you spend too much time seeking earthly pleasures, there is no room for spiritual growth. Your soul will only grow when you spend time studying my words and meditating on them. Everyone has 24 hours a day. Use it wisely. Use your time to be closer to me and build relationship with me. Worldly desires will be like thorns on a bush which will choke the growth of your soul. Choose me above everything else in this world. Drench in my living water so that your soul will bloom."

> Lord Jesus, help me to grow to be closer
> to you day by day and to choose you
> above every things else in this world.

REFLECTION: How much time do I spend seeking earthly treasures instead of spending time with the Lord?

YOUR EYES

*"Blessed are your eyes, because they see,
and your ears, because they hear."*

MATTHEW 13:16

In my vision I saw a person looking at his shadow. "My precious one, you have a body and a soul. Your eyes can see physical things in this world and your soul can see spiritual truth around you. Same with your ears. You can hear voices from near and far and you can hear me talking to you in your heart. Be attentive and be alert. The spiritual world is as real as your physical world. Not everyone realizes this. They live each day without my presence. But you know that I am always with you. Listen with your heart and you will see and hear me. Wisdom comes when you are with me."

*Thank you, Jesus, for opening my eyes to see you
and my ears to hear you more clearly each day.*

REFLECTION: Do I see with my spiritual eyes the presence of God everywhere I go?

MY SOUL THIRSTS

"O God, you are my God whom I seek; for you my flesh pines and my soul thirsts like the earth, parched, lifeless and without water."

PSALM 63:2

In my vision I saw a dry and parched land where everything was dying. When it rained plants began to grow and bloom. "My child, your soul needs my living water. The only way you will get it is to sit quietly and wait on me. You cannot rush around all day and expect that you will receive my living water. You need to sit still and call on my name and wait for the rain to fall on you. Only then you will be filled with the Holy Spirit which will quench your thirst and fill you with love, peace and joy. Come to the well and sit by my feet daily. Come and get filled, refreshed and renewed."

Give me, O Lord, your living water. My soul is thirsting for you day and night. Without you I will perish.

REFLECTION: Do I thirst for the living water that Jesus wants to give me to quench my soul?

REFORM YOUR WAYS

*"Reform your ways and your deeds, so that
I may remain with you in this place."*

JEREMIAH 7:3

In my vision I saw people all standing in the dark. One person started to sing and praise God and soon she became aglow with radiant light. Gradually others followed. One by one they all began to praise and worship God. Slowly they were all standing in the light. "My beloved, anyone who is in the dark must change and turn himself towards me. For I am the light of the world. If you heed my word and do as I have planned for you to do, your life will be transformed. When others see how peaceful and joyful you are, they will follow your example. Repent and reform, and you will be living in my light."

*Yes, Lord, I will reform my ways and confess my
sins. Fill me with your presence and your light.*

REFLECTION: Am I living in the light of Christ in my daily life? If not, have I repented?

WALK HUMBLY

> *"You have been told, O man, what is*
> *good, and what the Lord requires of you:*
> *Only to do the right and to love goodness,*
> *and to walk humbly with your God."*
>
> MICAH 6:8

In my vision I saw the disciples following Jesus on a dusty road. "My faithful one, to walk humbly is to always walk behind me and follow my footsteps. See what happened to Judas Iscariot? He walked ahead of me. He thought if he handed me over to the Pharisees they would know that I am the Messiah. He was acting on his own. He never asked me nor talked to me about his plan. Little did he know that I came into the world to suffer and to die on the cross so that you and everyone who believes in me will be saved. So be humble and always follow me wherever I am leading you."

Lord Jesus, I will follow you wherever you lead
me. Guide me and be with me till the end of time.

REFLECTION: Do I walk humbly and follow Jesus wherever he is leading me?

LACK OF FAITH

"He was not able to perform any mighty deed there, apart from curing a few sick people by laying his hands on them. He was amazed at their lack of faith."

MARK 6:5-6

In my vision I saw Jesus laying his hands on a few people who were sick. "My loving child, the more faith you have in me the more miracles I will be able to perform through you. Bring all those impossible cases to me and I will heal them. For it is my deepest desire to heal everyone physically, spiritually and emotionally. No one goes away empty-handed. You can trust in my healing power. For nothing is impossible for me. Many people do not receive healing because they ask not. Some are not healed because of their lack of faith in me."

Jesus, you are the healer and the miracle worker. With you all things are possible. Give me more faith in you, Lord.

REFLECTION: Do I have faith in Jesus that he can heal me with his healing power?

SIGN OF JONAH

> *"An evil and unfaithful generation seeks a sign, but no sign will be given it except the sign of Jonah the prophet."*
>
> MATTHEW 12:39

In my vision I saw Jesus at the temple teaching all those who want to hear him preach. "My child, I am the sign that will bring people closer to God my Father. Anyone who has ears to hear my word and believe in me will be saved. My word has power to change your heart and convert your life. Be attentive to me as the people in Nineveh did with Jonah the prophet. They listened to him and quickly repented and changed their ways. So must you if you want to enter into my kingdom. Seek me first and you will be saved. I am the sign that will set you free."

Lord Jesus, you are my savior and my redeemer. I believe that you came into the world to set us free.

REFLECTION: Do I listen to Jesus's teaching and try to repent for my sins and change my ways?

HEAVENLY BREAD

*"God rained manna upon them for food
and gave them heavenly bread."*

PSALM 78:24

I saw a white host inside a beautiful gold monstrance. "My precious one, every time when you eat my body and drink my blood you are transformed. Your body and my body are united as one. Every time when you visit me in church you will be filled with my presence and I will speak to your heart. This is my gift for you. Without me you have no life in you. With me you can change the world. Your heart will be filled with my love and will be able to do great things for the glory of God. Without me you will perish. I am the bread of life. Whoever eats my bread will have eternal life."

*My loving Jesus, I long to receive you into my
heart. Change me, mold me and transform
me into your image and likeness.*

REFLECTION: Do I hunger to receive the body and the blood of Christ who is the bread of life?

KINGDOM OF HEAVEN

"The kingdom of heaven is like yeast that a
woman took and mixed with three measures of
wheat flour until the whole batch was leavened."

MATTHEW 13:33

In my vision I saw people busy building a cathedral. Some were laying bricks, some were mixing cement. Everyone had a job in this project. "My faithful one, every little bit of your effort will help in building my kingdom. It takes a lot of people working together to make my kingdom a reality. Nothing is too small or insignificant. I can multiply your efforts like a little yeast leavening the whole batch of flour. So get moving and help me to make my kingdom a reality here on earth. All I need is your "yes" and your willingness to work. One day you will join me in my kingdom of heaven."

Lord Jesus, I want to help you build
your kingdom here on earth. Show
me what I need to do each day.

REFLECTION: Am I willing to say "yes" to Jesus and help him to build his kingdom of heaven here on earth?

HARVEST

> *"The harvest is the end of the age, and the harvesters are angels. Just as weeds are collected and burned up with fire, so will it be at the end of the age."*
>
> MATTHEW 13:39-40

In my vision I saw a field full of yellow colored plants and a farmer was cutting them with a long knife. "My child, at the end of the age everyone will be judged by me. Those who have done good deeds will be saved and those who have done evil in my Father's eyes will be condemned and burned. Be righteous and be loving for I am a merciful God and will only punish those who refuse to repent and follow me. They have chosen the wrong path and will be gathered like weeds and burned. Do good and avoid evil so that one day you will be with me in heaven."

> *Merciful Jesus, I am heartily sorry for all the times when I have not followed your commandments and done what you have asked me to do.*

REFLECTION: Am I doing good deeds and following Jesus daily instead of living a self-centered and sinful life?

RIGHTEOUS WILL SHINE

*"The righteous will shine like the sun
in the kingdom of their Father."*

MATTHEW 13:43

In my vision I saw the world from far away. Some areas had a lot of light, some were in darkness. "My precious one, everyone who does the will of my Father is a light in the world. Those who do not know me nor love me are in darkness. I am calling you to go and minister to them. Help them to come to the light. Bring joy and good news to them for I love everyone in this world. I long for the day when the whole world will be aglow. What joy that will bring to my heart! Go and be a light to those who are suffering and neglected. Bring healing and comfort to my people."

*Jesus, yes, I will go and bring the good news
to all those who are still in the darkness. Let
your light shine through me to others.*

REFLECTION: Do I bring comfort and healing to the people who are suffering and living in darkness?

THE LORD HEARS

*"For the Lord hears the poor, and does
not spurn those in bondage."*

PSALM 69:34

In my vision I saw a person begging outside the temple. "My child, every time when you cry out to me, I hear you. I know all your problems and sufferings. My heart goes out to everyone who cries out to me. For I am a merciful and loving God. I will be there for you. When I hear you cry, you can be assured of my help. Come to me for comfort and tell me everything that you are going through. You are my beloved and I care about you more than you will ever know. I am all ears and will answer your prayers. I will heal your broken heart. Do not lean on your own understanding. But trust on my wisdom."

*Lord Jesus, I know that you always
hear me. You answered all my prayers
and petitions. Thank you, Jesus.*

REFLECTION: Do I cry out to Jesus every time I am in trouble and ask for his help?

AUGUST

TREASURE

> *"The kingdom of heaven is like a treasure*
> *buried in a field, which a person finds and*
> *hides again, and out of joy goes and sells*
> *all that he has and buys that field."*
>
> MATTHEW 13:44

In my vision I saw Mary holding baby Jesus close to her heart. "My precious one, I am Mary's treasure. She gave up her life to fulfill my will. She was willing to lay down her life for me. According to the Jewish law she could have been stoned to death. You too are chosen to bring me into this world. I am your treasure also. When you put me first in your life you will be changed forever. You will be filled with my love and joy, and able to accomplish all that I have planned for you to do. Treasure me above everything else. For my love for you is infinite and eternal."

> *Yes, my loving Jesus, you are my treasure.*
> *You are more precious to me than*
> *gold or silver, family or friends.*

REFLECTION: Is Jesus my one and only treasure in this world?

GREED

*"Take care to guard against all greed,
for though one may be rich, one's life
does not consist of possessions."*

LUKE 12:15

In my vision I saw a man counting a pile of gold coins on the table. All of a sudden there was an earthquake and all the coins fell into the crack of the floor. "Yes, my child, do not get greedy. Money will not bring you happiness nor love. The most important thing in this life is to love and share what you have with others. This is a sure way to heaven. When you love others you cannot help but to share with those in need. Your wealth is a gift from God. Always be aware of others who are less fortunate than yourself. For every good deed you do in this world you will be rewarded a hundredfold in heaven."

*Lord Jesus, give me a generous heart so
that I will always be ready to share with
others what you have provided for me.*

REFLECTION: Am I willing to help those who are less fortunate than I am with my money, time and talent?

MOUTH

*"It is not what enters one's mouth that
defiles the man, but what comes out of
the mouth is what defiles one."*

MATTHEW 15:11

In my vision I saw an angel brought a coal and cleaned
the prophet's mouth. "My child, your mouth can praise
me or curse me. Your mouth has power to wound people's hearts or encourage others. Use your mouth wisely.
For every spoken word has power to kill or to love. Once
it is spoken you can never take it back. It will haunt you
or give you peace. So think before you speak. I have created the entire universe with my spoken word. You too
can change this world by speaking my word to others.
Use your mouth to build my kingdom here on earth and
you will be on the road to heaven."

*Help me, Lord, to use my mouth for
your honor and glory. Let every word
spoken by me be pleasing to you.*

REFLECTION: Do I use my mouth to praise and
encourage others as Jesus did for me?

MY LAW

> *"I will place my law within them, and write it upon their hearts. I will be their God, and they shall be my people."*
>
> JEREMIAH 31:33

In my vision I saw the word LOVE written in a heart shaped drawing. "Yes, my beloved, LOVE is my law. To love God with your whole heart, your whole mind and soul, and to love your neighbor as yourself is the law. My law will bring you love, peace and joy. Without my law there will be war, sadness and chaos. Anyone who puts love above everything else is living in my law. Those who have hatred, revenge and murderous thoughts are outside my law. They will suffer their consequences. Remember always have love in your heart and you will be holy and blameless in my sight."

> *I love you, Lord Jesus. Fill my heart with your love so that I will be a fountain of blessing to all the people around me.*

REFLECTION: Do I love God and all my neighbors as Jesus has loved me?

MIRACULOUS POWER

"Where did this man get this wisdom
and these miraculous powers?"

MATTHEW 13:54

In my vision I saw Jesus laid his hands on a dying person and he was totally healed. "My child, do you believe that I can perform miracles? Do you believe that I am the Son of the living God? I can do all things that my Father asks me to do. I came to save you and to heal you. Have expectant faith in me. When I went back to my hometown I could only heal a few people because of their lack of faith. No miracles took place there. When you come to me for healing have complete faith in me and you will be healed. Do not have doubt in your heart but have full confidence in my healing power."

Yes, Lord Jesus, you are my healer and my
redeemer. Nothing is impossible with you.
I believe in your miraculous power.

REFLECTION: Do I have faith in the healing power of Jesus and believe that he can even raise the dead?

HIS KINGSHIP

*"His kingship is an everlasting dominion
that shall not be taken away, his
kingship shall not be destroyed."*

In my vision I saw Jesus sitting on the throne with his mother Mary on his right. "My beloved, yes, I am King of kings and Lord of lords. But when you come to me in prayer I am always ready to listen and to be there for you. Do not be afraid to come to the throne with your requests. Come and spend time with me. I treasure every minute you are with me. You can confide in me. Ask anything from me and you will not go away empty handed. My mother is always ready to help you and to intercede for you. Open your eyes and see how we welcome you with loving arms. Come, my child, come."

*Praise you, Jesus. I love you and I adore
you. Come and reign in my heart and
in my mind. I am yours forever.*

REFLECTION: Am I afraid to go to the throne of God and ask Jesus for favors?

TWELVE WICKER BASKETS

"They all ate and were satisfied, and they picked up the fragments left over – twelve wicker baskets full."

MATTHEW 14:20

In my vision I saw a long table full of delicious food and drinks. "My child, I am a God of abundance. No one who comes to me will be hungry. For I love to lavish good things for my children. Have faith in me always. You will never lack anything when you are with me. See how generous I was with my disciples and the crowd of 5,000. They were all fed and were satisfied. They had 12 baskets full of leftovers. I will provide for all your needs. You will always have more than what you ask from me. Share with everyone around you and I will bless you abundantly. Ask and you shall receive."

My loving Jesus, you have always provided for all my needs. I feel so blessed. Help me to be generous with all those who are less fortunate than myself.

REFLECTION: Have I been generous in sharing what I have with those in need?

LORD SAVE ME

> *"'Lord, save me!' Immediately Jesus*
> *stretched out his hand and caught him."*
> MATTHEW 14:30-31

In my vision I saw Peter walking on water until he saw the storm and he started to sink. "My beloved, keep your eyes always on me and not on the storm. When you focus on the storm you too will sink into despair and hopelessness. When you are focusing on me you will have calm and peace. For nothing is impossible with me. You can trust me with all your heart. You will never drown nor perish. You are in my good hands. When you hold on to me nothing can snatch you away from me. You will have peace knowing that you are safe with me. So remember to call on me when you are in trouble."

> *Lord Jesus, you are my rock and my*
> *fortress. When I am with you I have no*
> *fear for I know that you are my savior.*

REFLECTION: Do I call on Jesus for help when I am in trouble?

VIGILANT

> *"Blessed are those servants whom the*
> *master finds vigilant on his arrival."*
>
> LUKE 12:37

In my vision I saw a servant standing by the door with a lantern in his hand looking out into the misty night. "My precious one, be prepared to welcome me when the time comes. Always have a light with you. Without my light you will not be able to see anything. With my light you will know how to live each day while you are waiting vigilantly for my coming. In the meantime work hard and share your goods with others. Always work with a smile on your face and joy in your heart. This way you will be spreading my love to everyone around you."

> *Loving Jesus, I wait patiently for the day*
> *when I will see you face to face. Fill me*
> *with more love and joy for everyone.*

REFLECTION: Am I prepared and eager to welcome Jesus into my heart?

GIVE YOU REST

> *"Come to me, all you who labor and are*
> *burdened, and I will give you rest."*
>
> MATTHEW 11:28

In my vision I saw myself resting on Jesus's shoulder. "My love, come into my arms and rest your head upon my shoulder. Hear my beating heart and the warmth of my love for you. Every time when you come to me, I will give you rest. You will be strengthened, renewed and refreshed every minute you spend with me. I cherish every moment when we are together. Just close your eyes and let your heart sing with joy. That is what I desire most from you. That is what I created you to be. Love me with all your heart, mind and soul. Spend time with me daily and you will find rest."

> *My precious Jesus, I want to be with you every*
> *day of my life. You are my Prince of Peace.*

REFLECTION: How often do I spend quiet time alone with Jesus and rest in his arms?

HUMBLE LIKE THIS CHILD

*"Whoever becomes humble like this child is
the greatest in the Kingdom of heaven."*

MATTHEW 18:4

In my vision I saw a loving father blessing his child and helping him to get ready to go to school. "Yes, my dear child, I will bless you each day when you come to me before you go out and do your work. Like a loving father I will see that no harm will come to you. If you listen to me and obey me I will bless you abundantly. Anyone who is obedient to my commandments will reap a good life. Whoever does not obey my statutes will wonder off and get into trouble. If you want to be the greatest in my Kingdom of heaven you must be faithful to my teachings and live humbly like a child."

*Loving Jesus, I will follow your commandments
and obey all your teachings. Protect me
and guide me so that one day I will be
with you in the Kingdom of heaven.*

REFLECTION: Am I living a humble and obedient life as a child of God?

CHEERFUL GIVER

*"Each must do as already determined,
without sadness or compulsion, for
God loves a cheerful giver."*

2 CORINTHIANS 9:7

In my vision I saw a child passing out roses to everyone. "My beloved, the more you give the more you will receive. Like the River Jordan which flows from the mountain to the Dead Sea. The river is full of fish and serves a purpose. Meanwhile at the end of the river lies the Dead Sea which has no outlets. The water flows to nowhere and becomes so salty that no living animals can survive there. This is what happens when one does not share what one has with others. The more you give the more I will bless you. So give generously and cheerfully to everyone around you."

*Thank you, Jesus, for reminding me to
be generous. Enlarge my heart so that
I will always be a cheerful giver.*

REFLECTION: Am I always ready to give to others as generously as God has blessed me?

DEMON CAME OUT

"Jesus rebuked him and the demon came out of him, and from that hour the boy was cured."

In my vision I saw a man chained to the tomb because he was possessed by a demon. "My child, if you have the faith of a mustard seed you will be able to do the things that I have asked my disciples to do. First you must believe that I have the authority to cast out demons. When you pray in my name I will give you the same power to overcome the evil one. So do not be afraid when someone comes to you for prayer. You can caste them out in my name which is a name above all names. Remember with me all things are possible. Just have complete faith in me."

Lord Jesus, I do believe that with you all things are possible. Give me the courage and the faith to pray with people when they need healing.

REFLECTION: Do I believe that Jesus has authority to caste out demons?

SEVEN TIMES

> *"Lord, if my brother sins against me, how often*
> *must I forgive him? As many as seven times?"*
> MATTHEW 18:21

In my vision I saw a person carrying a heavy load on his back walking very slowly as if in pain. "My child, whenever one carries unforgiveness in his heart, he is like the person in your vision. He can barely walk and carry out his daily chores. Unforgiveness is like poison one drinks hoping that the other person would die instead of himself. So be ready to forgive each day as I have forgiven you all your sins. Have no grudges, resentment and anger against anyone but love them as I have loved you. Do not let the sun go down on your anger. Be set free and ready to forgive always."

> *Merciful Jesus, please forgive me for all the times*
> *that I have anger and resentment in my heart.*
> *Help me to forgive others as you have forgiven me.*

REFLECTION: Is there anyone that I still have not yet forgiven? Do I have any anger and resentment in my heart?

FEVER LEFT HER

"He touched her hand, the fever left her,
and she rose and waited on him."

MATTHEW 8:15

In my vision I saw Jesus standing next to Peter's mother-in-law who was in bed and he touched her warm hand. "My love, every time when you are sick or tired, come to me and let me touch you and heal you. I will restore you to health and give you strength to move on. I am your healer and your savior. If you believe in my healing power, you will be healed. Have complete faith in me. Do you believe that I am the Son of the living God who have created you in your mother's womb? I loved you from the moment you were conceived. So do not hesitate to call on me in times of sickness."

My loving Jesus, I do believe in your
healing power. Please heal me and restore
me to health so that I will be able to do all
that you have planned for me to do.

REFLECTION: Have I asked Jesus to heal me when I was sick with fever?

GIVE THANKS

"Give thanks to the Lord, for he is good,
for his mercy endures forever."

PSALM 136:1

In my vision I saw a person kneeling in front of the altar thanking God for everything he had received. "My precious one, it is good to give thanks to everyone who has been a blessing in your life. But most of all you need to take time out of your busy life to thank me for all that I have done for you. When you give thanks your heart will be filled with joy and peace knowing how much I have loved you. In thanksgiving you will realize that I have provided and helped you every day of your life. A grateful heart is a joyful heart. The more you give thanks the more you will be blessed."

I praise you and thank you, O Lord. For you are
so good and merciful. I am forever grateful for all
the blessings that you have showered over me.

REFLECTION: Am I grateful for all my blessings and give thanks and praise to God daily?

MY SALVATION

*"Observe what is right, do what is
just, for my salvation is about to come,
my justice about to be revealed."*

ISAIAH 56:1

In my vision I saw people with parachutes landing safely on a grassy field. "My beloved child, when you are with me you will have no fear nor worry. For I will bring you safely to heaven. Like a parachute I will carry you home where I have prepared a banquet for you. Your salvation will be assured. Live each day doing what is right and just. Follow my commandments by loving each other as I have loved you. Do good and one day you will soon enjoy the fruit of your labor. Time is running short. Be prepared and be ready to meet me. That day will soon be here."

*My loving Jesus, I can hardly wait for that
day when I will be united with you forever in
heaven. You are my hope and my salvation.*

REFLECTION: Am I prepared and look forward to the day when I will be united with Jesus in heaven?

TO BE PERFECT

> *"If you wish to be perfect, go, sell what you have and give to the poor, and you will have treasure in heaven."*
>
> MATTHEW 19:21

In my vision Jesus was dressed in white teaching his disciples near the Sea of Galilee. "My child, it is not easy to be perfect. Only God is perfect. If you wish to improve yourself, then try to detach yourself from earthly things and concentrate on spiritual matters which will last forever. Earthly possessions will tarnish and break, but the spiritual treasures will last forever. Seek first the Kingdom of God and everything else will be given to you. Do not spend your energy and time accumulating earthly treasures. But be more compassionate and kind to all those who are in need."

> *Most precious Jesus, you are my treasure and my delight. Teach me to be more loving and caring especially towards those who are less fortunate than I am.*

REFLECTION: Do I seek the kingdom of God and try to detach myself from earthly possessions?

LABORERS

> *"The Kingdom of heaven is like a landowner who went out at dawn to hire laborers for his vineyard."*
>
> MATTHEW 20:1

In my vision I saw a farmer working in his vineyard. "My child, everyone is invited to work in my vineyard. Everything you do for me in my name will be fruitful. I will reward you a hundred fold. Do not worry when you see nothing is growing for a while. Everything takes time to mature and to flourish. Your job is to work hard for me even when the task seems so insignificant. I am not expecting you to do great things, but to do them with great love. You will not be judged by the result of your effort but by your willingness to follow my will. Are you ready to labor in my vineyard?"

> *Thank you, Lord Jesus, for calling me to be your laborer. I will go and work in your vineyard.*

REFLECTION: Am I ready to obey and to work for Jesus in his vineyard?

LAST WILL BE FIRST

"Many who are first will be last,
and the last will be first."

MATTHEW 19:30

In my vision I saw a shepherd carrying a little lamb over his shoulder and walking ahead of all the other sheep. "My beloved, anyone who is willing to follow me will enter into my kingdom. Those who are too weak or unable to walk, I will personally carry them. It is not how wise or how capable you are, but those who are humble and need me will enter into my kingdom first. Always remember to ask for my help. Never think of yourself as one who can do it all by your own ability. Only those who are humble and trust in my mercy and power will be saved."

Lord Jesus, you are my good shepherd. Without your help I can do nothing. Hold me tight and never let me be separated away from you.

REFLECTION: Do I try to be humble and trust in Jesus' mercy and his saving power?

MY SHEEP

> *"My sheep were scattered over the whole earth, with no one to look after them or to search for them."*
>
> Ezekiel 34:6

In my vision I saw a sheep amongst a thorny bush. It was lost and was crying for help. "My precious one, so many of my sheep are helpless. I need you to find them and to lead them back to me. They do not know the way to salvation. They have no one to help them get out of their thorny situations. They are lost and forgotten. Go and be their shepherd and lead them back to the right path. They are blind and do not see my light. They need your assistance. Go and show them the narrow way so that they too will live an abundant life with me here on earth and in heaven."

> *My most compassionate Jesus, show me all those lost sheep who need my help so that I can bring them back to you.*

REFLECTION: Am I ready to be a shepherd to those who have wandered away from the right path?

NEW HEART

> *"I will give you a new heart and place a new spirit within you, taking from your bodies your stony hearts and giving you natural hearts."*
>
> EZEKIEL 36:26

In my vision I saw a surgeon taking out an old heart and replacing it with a new red heart. "I will give my heart to you. From now on you will be able to love others as I have loved you. You will see people with my eyes and feel with my mercy and compassion for them. Your heart and mine will beat as one. I will open your heart so that you will be able to love those who are lonely and depressed. I will give you words of love and understanding so that you will be able to comfort those who are weeping and mourning. Your heart will rejoice with them and love them as I love you."

> *O loving Jesus, fill my stony heart with your love.*
> *Thank you for giving me a new heart so that I*
> *will be able to love others as you have loved me.*

REFLECTION: Do I desire to receive a new heart and a new spirit from Jesus?

WEDDING FEAST

> *"The Kingdom of heaven may be likened to a*
> *king who gave a wedding feast for his son."*
>
> MATTHEW 22:2

In my vision I saw myself dressed all in white sitting next to Jesus at the head of the table in a wedding feast. "My beloved, you are my spouse. I have chosen you to be with me in heaven. When you are ready to enter into my Kingdom I will prepare for you a big banquet to welcome you. You will be surrounded by all your loved ones and your tears will be wiped away with joy. I will welcome you into my loving arms and bring you to my Father in heaven. You will sit by me and enjoy the feast. For you are mine and I will always cherish you. Come into my Kingdom of heaven."

> *My most loving Jesus, I long to be in your*
> *arms and sit with you to enjoy the wedding*
> *feast one day. You are the love of my life.*

REFLECTION: Do I look forward to the day when I will enjoy the wedding feast in the Kingdom of heaven?

NO DUPLICITY

> *"Jesus saw Nathanael coming toward him and said, 'Here is a true Israelite. There is no duplicity in him.'"*
>
> JOHN 1:47

In my vision I saw a person holding a mask in front of his face pretending he was someone else. "My loving child, you do not have to put a mask on for me to love you. For I know what is in your heart and mind. I know what you are going to say before you even open your mouth. I know when you are sleeping or waking. I know all your thoughts. So be honest with me and with yourself. Like Nathanael, you can speak your mind to me. Pour out your heart to me when you pray. I love an honest person who has no duplicity in him. Be sincere and be truthful always."

> *Thank you, Jesus, for loving me the way I am. You know me so well. I can be open and honest with you at all times.*

REFLECTION: Am I honest with Jesus and sincere and truthful with others?

BLIND PHARISEE

*"Blind Pharisee, cleanse first the inside of the
cup, so that the outside also may be clean."*

MATTHEW 23:26

In my vision I saw a person sweeping out dirt from his house with a bloom. "My child, your soul is like your house. You need to clean out all your sins and wrong-doings from time to time. Preferably daily. This way your inside is as clean as your outside. Do you not take a shower and wash your face every day? So you must also cleanse your inside daily. Examination of conscience is one of the best ways to change your behavior. See your-self as I see you. Know that I will wash you clean if you repent and ask forgiveness. There is no sin so great that I will not forgive. So do not be afraid to come to me."

*Wash me clean, Lord Jesus, from every
sin that I have committed against you
in the past. Help me to always be ready
to repent and return to you daily.*

REFLECTION: How often do I try to examine my conscience and ask Jesus to forgive my sins?

SERVE THE LORD

"As for me and my household,
we will serve the Lord."

JOSHUA 24:15

In my vision I saw myself wearing a white apron and carrying a tray of drinks to serve people around me. "My faithful one, when you serve others you are serving me. Every action you do for me will bring glory to my Father in heaven. Do each job with love and your reward will be great in heaven. Do it with compassion and mercy. Serve especially those who have no one to help them, those who are poor and sick, those who are helpless and those who are not easy to love. They need my mercy and compassion. Whenever you do acts of kindness to the least of your brothers you are doing it to me."

Jesus, my love, to serve you is my delight.
Enlarge my heart so that I will be able to
serve others as you have done for me.

REFLECTION: Am I willing to serve those who are sick and helpless with love and compassion?

ANGELS OF GOD

> *"Amen, amen, I say to you, you will see the*
> *sky opened and the angels of God ascending*
> *and descending on the Son of Man."*
>
> JOHN 1:51

In my vision I saw Jesus ascending into heaven with angels on his left and right radiating with glorious light. "My precious one, it takes spiritual eyes to see the spiritual world. Not everyone can see angels. It is a gift from God. Blessed are the eyes that can see and the ears that can hear. Angels are always present in this world. They play an important role in guiding and protecting you. Every angel has a job to do. They bring your prayers to the Throne Room. They are with you always especially when you need them most. Remember to ask them for protection and guidance everywhere you go."

> *Thank you, Jesus, for revealing to me that*
> *I have angels from heaven who are always*
> *ready to help me and to guide me.*

REFLECTION: Am I aware that my guardian angel is protecting me everywhere I go?

STAY AWAKE

> *"Stay awake! For you do not know on*
> *which day your Lord will come."*
>
> MATTHEW 24:42

In my vision I saw a soldier standing at attention ready to carry out any orders that he was called to do. "My little one, be ready and prepare your soul to meet me. Every day examine your conscience before you go to bed at night and see if you are truly living each day for my honor and glory. For the time is running short. Soon I will be coming again. Be prepared and be ready to receive me. It will be a joyful day for all those who are ready to receive me. Rejoice and be glad that my Kingdom is coming soon. Sing praise and thanksgiving daily!"

> *Lord, help me to prepare to live each day as*
> *my last day here on earth. I look forward*
> *to the day when you will come again.*

REFLECTION: Do I have expectant faith and joyfully look forward to the day when I will see Jesus face to face?

ROCK OF REFUGE

"Be my rock of refuge, a stronghold to give me safety; for you are my rock and my fortress."

PSALM 71:3

In my vision I saw myself hiding in a cave. "My precious child, as long as you are under my wings you have nothing to fear. For I have come to overcome all evil. Do not worry about tomorrow but live each day by staying close to me. Always feel safe in the palm of my hand. No evil one can snatch you away from me. You can sleep well every night knowing that your guardian angel is always with you and my watchful eyes are upon you. Like a mother hen I will protect you from all harm. You can rest in peace and know that I will never leave you nor forsake you."

O Lord Jesus, you are my rock and my fortress. With you by my side I have nothing to fear. Jesus, I trust in you.

REFLECTION: Do I run to Jesus for help every time then I am afraid or worried?

LORD OF PEACE

"May the Lord of peace himself give you
peace at all times and in every way."

2 THESSALONIANS 3:16

In my vision I saw myself sitting in front of a large crucifix and focusing on the suffering of Christ. "Peace I give to you, not as the world gives. For I am the Prince of Peace and the Lord of lords. When you are with me, you will have deep peace beyond your understanding. Even though everything around you seems to be falling apart, when you are in my presence, you will feel peace. You will not have fear nor anxiety. Be still and know that I am God. I have overcome all evil and will protect you from all harm. You can count on me. Nothing will disturb your peace when you are in my presence."

Loving Jesus, you are my Prince of
Peace. Fill my heart with your peace.
With you I know all will be well.

REFLECTION: Do I believe that when I am with Jesus all my anxiety and fear will be replaced by his peace?

STAND FIRM

> *"Therefore stand firm and hold fast to the tradition that you were taught, either by an oral statement or by a letter of ours."*
>
> 2 THESSALONIANS 2:15

In my vision I saw Jesus standing with his hands tied behind him standing in front of the Pontius Pilate. "Beloved, when people accuse you of something that is not true, do not be angry or feel abandoned. Stand firm and know that I will be standing next to you. Hold fast to what you believe and the truth will set you free. So do not worry about what you need to say or how to defend yourself. I will give you the words of wisdom when you speak. I will open their eyes to see the truth. You can be sure of this. Have courage and hope in me. I will always be there with you."

> *Lord Jesus, thank you for your words of encouragement. Help me to stand firm and hold fast to the truth.*

REFLECTION: Do I have the courage to stand firm in the truth when people falsely accuse me?

SEPTEMBER

NOT IN DARKNESS

"But you are not in darkness, for that day to overtake you like a thief. For all of you are children of the light and children of the day."

1 THESSALONIANS 5:4-5

In my vision I saw a lot of tiny bugs that are aglow in the dark of the night. "My little one, the darker the world, the more your soul will glow in my light. For I am the light of the world. The more time you spend with me, the more light you will have. Without my light you will walk in darkness and fumble. With my light you will bring joy and hope to others. See how little children are delighted when they see the tiny bugs aglow in their backyard? It brings such joy into their hearts. You are the light that shines in this darkened world now. Let my light shine through you."

Thank you, Jesus, for being my light. May your light shine through me for I am a child of God.

REFLECTION: Do I remember to bring love and joy to others with the light of Christ within me?

MERCY OF GOD

"I, like a green olive tree in the house of God,
trust in the mercy of God forever and ever."

PSALM 52:10

In my vision I saw myself as an olive tree planted next to a stream of water that kept my leaves green. The water flew out of the temple and it never became dry. It washed away all the dirt and insects away from my trunk; and it quenched my thirst. "My love, stay close to me and I will pour my mercy upon you. You will be refreshed and renewed by my forgiveness and compassion. You will be washed clean by my living water. When the drought comes, you will not perish. For I will always love you and will bless you whenever you turn your heart back to me."

My Jesus, thank you for pouring your mercy
and compassion upon me. Never let me be
separated away from your loving heart.

REFLECTION: Am I planted next to the living water of Jesus and let his mercy and compassion flow into my heart?

TALENTS

> *"To one he gave five talents; to another two; to a third, one – to each according to his ability."*
>
> MATTHEW 25:15

In my vision I saw all different kinds of flowers in a garden. Some are small and some are large. Each one is different. "My child, I created each one of you unique. Some I gave more talents than others. But everyone is perfect in my eyes. You who are given much, more is expected from you. Never judge others. No one is created with the same amount of talents and abilities. The important thing to remember is that you need to use your talents that I have given you. Your talents are for the good of others. Do not be afraid to use them. Everyone is called to build my Kingdom here on earth."

> *O Lord, thank you for giving me so many talents and blessings. Help me to always ready to use my talents for the good of others.*

REFLECTION: Have I used my talents that God has given me for the benefit of others?

FORFEIT HIS LIFE

*"What profit would there be for one to gain
the whole world and forfeit his life."*

MATTHEW 16:26

In my vision I saw a person trying to hang himself. "My beloved, your life is the most precious gift I have given you. Yet many people do not treasure it and try to destroy oneself. Do you know that without life you can do nothing? And yet so many people in this world choose money and fame before living a good and peaceful life. There is no greater gift I can give you than your life here on earth. Enjoy each day and know that I am loving you always. You are never alone or helpless. With me there is hope and a future. Treasure me above everything else and you will live an abundant and joyful life."

*My loving Jesus, I am forever grateful for you
in my life. Without you, life is meaningless.
With you I have peace, love and joy.*

REFLECTION: Do I treasure my life here on earth and live an abundant and joyful life by serving God?

NEW WINE

"New wine must be poured into fresh wineskins."
LUKE 5:38

In my vision I saw Jesus turning water into wine at the wedding of Cana after his mother Mary told him that they were running out of wine. "My child, I am the new wine. I came to lead you on a new path -- a path filled with sacrificial love and suffering. Following my commandments and statues are good, but following my agape love is even more superior. For love covers all sins and faults. I poured out my blood and water to wash you clean. This way you will have a clean heart and be transformed into my image and likeness. Be new wine to others as I have been for you."

Lord, mold me and change my heart so that I will be more loving and forgiving as you are to me.

REFLECTION: Do I imitate Jesus and try to be a new wine for others with love and compassion?

I MUST PROCLAIM

*"To the other towns also I must proclaim the
good news of the kingdom of God, because
for this purpose I have been sent."*

LUKE 4:43

In my vision I saw Jesus walking along a dusty road with
his disciples to the next town. "Beloved, my main purpose in life was to bring the good news to the people.
This is also your mission. I need your hands and feet
to go out and to proclaim the kingdom of God. Do not
worry about what to say or what to do. I will be with
you every step of the way. You will be guided by the
Holy Spirit and the doors will open for you wherever
you are led to go. All I need is your willing heart to carry
out my will. I will provide for all your needs. Fear not
and know that I am always with you."

*Guide me, O Lord, to the right path where you
want me to go and to proclaim your good news to
others. Give me the courage to carry out your will.*

REFLECTION: Is it my mission to bring good news to
the people who are searching for God?

SING PRAISE

"Sing praise to the Lord with lyre, with the lyre and melodious song."

PSALM 98:5

In my vision I saw King David singing, dancing and rejoicing. "My precious one, every time when you praise me it is like music to my ears. You do not know how much joy it brings me when you are happy with a grateful heart. It is like watching a child running towards her parent with a big smile. When you sing joyfully to me, my heart leaps with joy. So take time each day to praise and to thank me. A joyful heart will give you a sound mind and a healthy heart. The evil ones will flee because they come to destroy and to kill. Never forget to praise and to give thanks for everything I have given you."

I love to start each day singing praises and giving thanks to you, Lord Jesus. You are the joy of my life.

REFLECTION: Do I sing and praise Jesus for everything he has given me each day?

JESUS

"She will give birth to a son, and you are to give him the name Jesus, because he will save his people from their sins."

MATTHEW 1:21

In my vision I saw a priest blessing a person saying, "In the name of Jesus, you are forgiven." "My child, my name has power. It can save you from your sins and give you peace and serenity. So say my name often throughout the day. It will bring you closer to me. It will set you free from all your worries and anxieties. There is power in my name. Whenever you say my name Jesus, I will be there for you. I will protect you from all harm. My name has power to overcome all evil. Praise my name day and night and your heart with be filled with my love and peace."

Jesus, Jesus, Jesus, you are my rock and my salvation. May your name be praised forever and ever, Amen.

REFLECTION: How often do I say the name of Jesus and thank him for saving me from all my sins?

TOUCH HIM

> *"Everyone in the crowd sought to touch him because power came forth from him and healed them all."*
>
> LUKE 6:19

In my vision I saw Jesus standing with radiant light. A leper came towards Jesus and as soon as he touched Jesus' garment, he was healed and filled with light. "My child, do not be afraid to come close to me and touch me. I came into this world so that everyone can touch me and be healed. I want to set this world aglow with the fire of my healing love. Be my light to everyone and I will give you the power to heal their illnesses. Reach out and touch them as you have been touched by me. All things are possible when you pray in my name."

> *Lord Jesus, transform my heart so that I will have the courage and the faith to go out and share your healing touch with others.*

REFLECTION: Am I hesitant to go close to Jesus and touch him so that he can heal me?

BLESSED ARE YOU

*"Blessed are you when people hate you, and when
they exclude and insult you, and denounce your
name as evil on account of the Son of Man."*

LUKE 6:22

In my vision I saw Jesus dressed all in a white garment
and he reached out his hands to save those who were
covered with mud in a pond. "My precious one, do not
be afraid when people ill treat you because of me. I will
always come and rescue you. I will cleanse you from all
insults and abuse because of my name. Have no hatred in
your heart but fill your heart with my love, compassion
and forgiveness. Only through suffering and endurance
will you be saved. See how much I have endured on the
cross for you. Pray for those who persecute you and you
will be blessed abundantly in heaven."

*Loving Jesus, be with me when others
hate me because of you. Strengthen me
when I am weak and give me the courage
to continue to be faithful to you.*

REFLECTION: Do I pray for those who persecute me
instead of having hatred in my heart for them?

RAISED WITH CHRIST

*"If then you were raised with Christ,
seek what is above, where Christ is
seated at the right hand of God."*

COLOSSIANS 3:1

In my vision I saw myself floating upward towards the sky with Jesus by my side. "My love, you no longer belong to this world. Seek first the kingdom of God and everything else with be given to you. Do not worry about what to eat or what to wear; your heavenly Father will provide for all your needs. Grow closer to me with prayer and fasting. See the world with my eyes and do all that I have planned for you to do. Focus on me and I will raise your thoughts towards heaven. Do not waste your time preserving things that will perish in this world. But focus on spending eternal life with me in heaven."

*My precious Jesus, help me to always seek
you first above everything else and to desire
earnestly to enter into your kingdom one day.*

REFLECTION: How much time do I spend seeking God instead of worrying about worldly events and my own needs?

GOD'S CO-WORKERS

*"For we are God's co-workers; you
are God's field, God's building."*

1 CORINTHIANS 3:9

In my vision I saw people sowing, planting and watering in the field. "My beloved, I called you to work in my vineyard. You are chosen to do a specific chore. Each one is given different talents and gifts and each one has a role in building my kingdom. Spend time alone with me each day and you will be guided to do all that I have planned for you each day. Remember my yoke is easy and my burden light. When you do the things that you are called to do, it will give you great peace and joy. For this is the purpose of your life: to do the will of my Father."

*Lord Jesus, I want to live each day
doing your Father's will. Let me never
lose sight of the purpose of my life.*

REFLECTION: Am I a co-worker in building God's kingdom here on earth?

GOOD PERSON

> *"A good person out of the store of goodness in his heart produces good, but an evil person out of a store of evil produces evil; for the fullness of the heart the mouth speaks."*
>
> LUKE 6:45

In my vision I saw a three-tiered fountain with water flowing from one level to another. "My loving child, so it is with your heart. When your heart is overflowing with my love, you will be able to love others as I love you. You will produce much fruit. For love can move mountains. You can heal people with my love, give hope to those who are helpless, and comfort those who need to hear the words of encouragement and mercy. Let your heart be filled with my love and compassion each morning so that your fountain will never run dry."

Fill my heart with more of your love, Lord. I want to be a good person who can bless everyone who comes into my life each day.

REFLECTION: Is my heart filled with love and compassion of Jesus ready to share with everyone around me?

BELIEVES IN HIM

"For God so loved the world that he gave his only son, so that everyone who believes in him might not perish but might have eternal life."

JOHN 3:16

In my vision I saw myself kneeling in front of a cross. "My beloved, do you believe that I have power to save you through my cross? Yes, that was the main purpose why I came into this world. I came not to condemn but to save. Everyone who believes in me will be saved. Like those Jews in the desert who looked upon the bronze serpent did not die of poison but lived. My child, bring others to my cross and show them how much I love them even through death on the cross. There is no greater love than one who lays down one's life for others. Tell this good news to everyone you meet each day."

Most loving Jesus, thank you for dying on the cross for us. I will tell everyone who does not know you nor believes in you.

REFLECTION: Do I believe that I will be saved because Jesus died on the cross for my sins?

BEHOLD YOUR MOTHER

> *"'Behold your mother.' And from that hour*
> *the disciple took her into his home."*
>
> JOHN 19:27

In my vision I saw Mary standing at the foot of the cross. "My child, I am giving my mother to you. Invite her into your home and your heart. She is your mother as much as she is mine. She will intercede for all your needs. She will stand by you throughout all your suffering and trials. For she loves you as much as she loves me and she knows your heart. See how faithful she was when I was dying on the cross? She never left me like my disciples did. My mother never gave up on me. You can call on her and she will never abandon you but will pray for you as she did for me."

> *Thank you, Jesus, for giving me your*
> *mother. Mary, remember me in times of*
> *need. Pray for me so that I will be able to*
> *love Jesus more and more each day.*

REFLECTION: Have I asked Mary our mother to teach me how to love Jesus like she did?

ONE MEDIATOR

*"There is also one mediator between
God and men, the man Christ Jesus,
who gave himself as ransom for all."*

1 TIMOTHY 2:5-6

In my vision I saw a prison door opened and a prisoner
was set free. "My precious child, I have paid a steep price
to set you free from all your sins. I have suffered and
died on the cross so that you may have an abundant
life. I love you so much that I am willing to lay down
my life for you. I want to spend eternity with you in
heaven. I am your mediator and redeemer. You belong
to me. Therefore live each day with a grateful heart. Let
thanksgiving be always on your lips. Treat others as I
have treated you with love and compassion. Sing praise
and be grateful."

*O most loving and precious Jesus, I want to
thank you for being my mediator and savior.
May you be praised and glorified forever.*

REFLECTION: Have I thanked and praised Jesus for
being my mediator and redeemer?

FAITH, HOPE, LOVE

"So faith, hope, love remains, these three;
but the greatest of these is love."

1 CORINTHIANS 13:13

In my vision I saw a large hand holding a heart with a cross on top of it and a sword piercing the heart. "My little one, love is all that matters. If you have faith in me but do not have love, you cannot be my disciple. If you have hope for the future but do not have love, your life will be lived in vain. Love is patient. Love is kind. Love endures all things. So live each day with love in your heart for me and for everyone especially for those less fortunate than yourself. Only in this way you will have a joyful and meaningful life."

O most sacred heart of Jesus, fill my heart
with more of your love so that I will be able
to love others as you have loved me.

REFLECTION: Do I live each day with love in my heart for everyone, especially those who are neglected and forgotten?

THIS GENERATION

*"To what shall I compare the people of
this generation? What are they like?"*

LUKE 7:31

In my vision I saw young people dancing and having a great time and not worried about anything. "My child, this generation lives in a fantasy world. They are only concerned about having a good time. They are not aware that they have a purpose in life and their time in this world is very short. Everything revolves around their own pleasure. My precious one, you know that this world is not your permanent home. You work hard to bring the truth to them. But they are not ready to listen to you. Do not give up. Pray for them constantly. Be an example for them and stand firm in your faith."

*Lord Jesus, give me the wisdom on
how to be a model for this generation.
Help me to lead them back to you.*

REFLECTION: Do I pray and act as a model for this generation who has no faith in Jesus?

LOVE OF MONEY

> *"For the love of money is the root of all evils, and some people in their desire for it have strayed from the faith and have pierced themselves with many pains."*
>
> 1 TIMOTHY 6:10

In my vision I saw rich people riding in a convertible and there were dollar bills falling down from the buildings. "My beloved, do not seek money and fame. See how those rich and famous people were cheered one day and hated in the turn of events. They have no life within them. It is all vanity. My love, seek first my kingdom and you will have an abundant life. I will bless and shower you with peace and joy beyond your imagination. You will be carried in the palms of my hands. You will be treasured and honored by the people around you. Desire me above all else."

Yes, Lord Jesus Christ, you are the center of my life. I love you with all my heart, mind and soul.

REFLECTION: Do I seek the kingdom of God instead of wealth and fame?

SPIRITUAL BODY

*"If there is a natural body, there
is also a spiritual body."*

1 Corinthians 15:44

In my vision I saw Jesus standing in front of his disciples after his resurrection. They were so surprised that he came in through the locked door. "My beloved, one day you too will have a spiritual body like mine. You will be able to walk through locked doors and rise above the ground. Like my mother Mary you will be radiant with light and glow like the moon. Your spiritual body can take you wherever you want to go and soar like an eagle. You will be able to stand on a cloud and see the world from above. Eyes have not seen and ears have not heard what I have prepared for you in heaven."

*My most beloved Jesus, I long for the day when
I will have a spiritual body like yours and be
able to spend eternity with you in heaven.*

REFLECTION: Do I look forward to the day when I will have a spiritual body like Jesus?

SEEK THE LORD

> *"Seek the Lord while he may be found, call him while he is near."*
> ISAIAH 55:6

In my vision I saw a little boy playing hide and seek. "My child, just because I am not visible to your naked eyes does not mean that I am not near. Remember the time when you were playing hide and seek with your children? What joy it was when your child finally found you. That is the same when you seek me. There is joy and rejoicing when you seek me with all your heart. Look for me often. Look for me in everyone's face you meet each day. Look for me in the least expected places. Let the joy reign in your heart when you finally find me."

> *Lord Jesus, I long to see your face. Help me to seek you everywhere I go.*

REFLECTION: Do I remember to take time to search and seek the face of Jesus daily?

TWO MASTERS

"No servant can serve two masters. He will either hate one and love the other, or be devoted to one and despise the other. You cannot serve God and mammon."

LUKE 16:13

In my vision I saw a person standing between two rooms. One was dark but in the corner there was a pile of gold and the other was bright with a radiant light. "My little one, many people think they can be in both rooms and have it all. But in reality you can only be either in the dark or in the light. You cannot have your heart divided between God and money. When you make choices in your life is money your main concern or God? You cannot serve two masters. When your eyes are upon wealth, be assured that your back will be against me. Choose me and you will have an abundant and joyful life."

Lord Jesus, help me to love you above everything else. Give me the wisdom to choose you always in every decision I make.

REFLECTION: Is God my only master or do I spend all my time and energy on my career and making money?

WISDOM

*"The wisdom that comes from heaven
is first of all pure; then peace-loving,
considerate, submissive, full of mercy and
good fruit, impartial and sincere."*

JAMES 3:17

In my vision I saw Jesus teaching his disciples with one hand holding the scripture and the other pointing up towards his Father. "My precious one, I am the seed of wisdom. Whoever believes in me will follow me and imitate all that I do. My heart is pure and always ready to do my Father's will. I came to love and not to condemn but to have mercy on all those who need forgiveness. My heart goes out to everyone for I am impartial to all God's children. I am sincere and considerate. Imitate me and you will be saved. Stay pure and peace-loving. Only in this way you will be truly my disciple."

*Loving Jesus, fill me with your wisdom and
mercy for others. I want to imitate you in
everything I do for your glory Lord.*

REFLECTION: Do I try to follow and imitate Jesus, who is the seed of wisdom?

278   LILY L. LOH

POWER AND AUTHORITY

*"Jesus summoned the twelve and gave them
power and authority over all demons and to
cure diseases, and he sent them to proclaim
the kingdom of God and to heal the sick."*

LUKE 9:1-2

In my vision I saw lightning, rain, storm and thunder outside the window. "My child, I am the creator of this entire universe. I have power to control the storm and the sea. I am giving you authority to go out to proclaim the good news to all who have ears to hear. I will give you the power to heal the sick and to caste out demons. All I need from you is your willingness to step out and go wherever I send you. I will give you everything you need to do the job. Have no worry nor anxiety whatsoever. I will be with you wherever I lead you. You can be sure of that."

*O Lord, give me the courage to step out of
my comfort zone. I want to be your disciple
and go wherever you are leading me.*

REFLECTION: Am I aware that Jesus has given me power and authority to go out and to do his work?

GOD IS FAITHFUL

*"God is faithful and will not let you be
tried beyond your strength; but with the
trial he will also provide a way out, so
that you may be able to bear it."*

1 CORINTHIANS 10:13

In my vision I saw a person dragging a large crate with difficulty. "My love, everyone will experience trials in his life. But be assured that you will never be alone during a trial. I will be helping you step by step. You need not be discouraged. I will give you strength to go through every trial in your life. You will develop patience, endurance and compassion for others who are going through their trials. You will be wiser and become more dependent on me as you grow in maturity through your trials. So have confidence in me and know that I am faithful and will always be there for you."

*Thank you, Jesus, for your words of comfort
and assurance. I know you are a faithful
God and will always provide a way out.*

REFLECTION: Do I have confidence in Jesus that he will give me the strength to go through all trials?

NAKED I CAME

> *"Naked I came forth from my mother's womb and naked shall I go back again. The Lord gave and the Lord has taken away; blessed be the name of the Lord!"*
>
> JOB 1:21

In my vision I saw a woman lying in a casket with a rosary in her hand. "My beloved, when you die you will take nothing into heaven except your love for me and for others. The treasures that you have stored in heaven will never rust nor tarnish. In heaven you will have everything you need. What you have accumulated here on earth is useless in heaven except for all the good works you have done for others. So spend each day doing good instead of hogging material things for yourself. Only love matters in heaven. Live each day loving and helping others. Then you will have treasures in heaven."

Lord Jesus, you are my treasure. I want to live each day loving and serving you.

REFLECTION: Have I been storing treasures in heaven instead of this world?

CURING DISEASES

> *"Then they set out and went from village*
> *to village proclaiming the good news*
> *and curing diseases everywhere."*
>
> LUKE 9:6

In my vision I saw the disciples laying hands on the sick and they were cured. "My faithful one, I am sending you to proclaim the good news and to cure the sick as I have sent my disciples. Do not worry what to say or what to do. I will give you the power and the wisdom to carry out my mission. All I need is your cooperation. For I have a plan for you: a plan to prosper you and give you a fruitful life. Have courage to carry out what I have planned for you to do. All I need is your "yes" and your willingness to do my will. You will see miracles and healings beyond your expectation."

> *Yes, Lord Jesus, I will follow you and go out*
> *to proclaim the good news and to cure the*
> *sick. Give me the courage to do your will.*

REFLECTION: Am I willing to carry out what Jesus has planned for me to do, preaching the good news and curing the sick?

GOD'S MESSIAH

> *"'Who do you that say I am?' Peter*
> *answered, 'God's Messiah.'"*
>
> LUKE 9:20

In my vision I saw Jesus all aglow on the mount of transfiguration. "My beloved, yes, I am God's Messiah. Do you believe that I am the Son of God who came down into the world to save you? I came to die on the cross for all your sins. There is no greater love than the one who lays down his life for another. True love requires suffering and sacrifice. I came to set you free and to give you eternal life in heaven. You will have total bliss. Eyes have not seen and ears have not heard what I have prepared for you. So from now on do everything for my honor and glory and your reward will be great in heaven."

> *Lord Jesus, you are King of kings and Lord*
> *of lords. You are our Messiah sent by God.*
> *You alone will I worship and adore.*

REFLECTION: Do I truly believe that Jesus is the God's Messiah sent from heaven?

MICHAEL

> *"War broke out in heaven; Michael and his angels battled against the dragon."*
>
> REVELATION 12:7

In my vision I saw the angel St. Michael all dressed in armor ready to do battle. "My child, fear not. My angels St. Michael, St. Gabriel and St. Raphael are always with you. They will help you in fighting the war against the evil one. You are never alone. Call for their help often. They will protect you from all harm. They will conquer the evil one when you are being tempted. Ask them to assist you. They will not leave you but always be ready to guide you and guard you every day of your life. Thank them often for all that they have done for you."

> *Loving Jesus, please send St. Michael and all the other angels to be with me each day as I go about doing God's will. Ask them to protect me from the evil one.*

REFLECTION: Have I asked Jesus to send the angels to protect me from all harm?

LEFT BEHIND

"No one who sets a hand to the plow and looks to what was left behind is fit for the kingdom of God."

In my vision I saw Lot's wife turning back to look at the city where she lived before and suddenly turned into a pillar of salt. "My little one, never live in the past if you want to enter into the kingdom of God. Look forward and follow me each day. The past is gone and you will not have life in the present if you keep on looking back. But if you follow me day by day and help me to build my kingdom here on earth then you will have a bright future in heaven. You will be richly blessed and rewarded by my Father who loves you as much as I love you."

I will follow you, Jesus, and try not to look back. I want to dedicate myself to helping you to build your kingdom here on earth.

REFLECTION: Do I live in the present with Jesus instead of always looking back to the past?

OCTOBER

YOU KNOW ME

*"O lord, you have probed me and you know
me, you know when I sit and I stand."*

PSALM 139:1-2

In my vision I saw myself sitting next to Jesus watching my life being shown on a big screen. "My child, I am with you every minute of your life. You are never alone. I know you better than anyone else in this world. I know your deepest thoughts especially when you think you are totally alone. I know when you are happy or sad, sitting or standing. I know every movement of your body. I even know before you speak what you are going to say or do. Feel my presence and live each day as if I am right next to you and you will never regret anything you do or say in your life."

*Thank you, Jesus, for this beautiful vision.
Help me to remember that I am never alone
and you are always with me by my side.*

REFLECTION: Do I feel the presence of Jesus close to me throughout the day?

ANGELS

*"The Lord has put angels in charge of
you, to guard you in all your ways."*

PSALM 91:11

In my vision I saw an important person walking down the street with a bodyguard right next to him. "My beloved, you too have a bodyguard right next to you at all times. Your guardian angel watches you everywhere you go. He checks out the surroundings before you get into trouble. He alerts you whenever there is danger. He helps you to avoid all evil and prompts you to do the right thing at the right time. You are never alone because your angel is always by your side. This is his duty and his job. Listen to your guardian angel and you will be safe."

*Lord, you thought of everything. Thank you
for giving me a guardian angel to protect me
from all harm. I feel so safe and loved.*

REFLECTION: Have I thanked Jesus for giving me a guardian angel to protect me at all times?

YOUR STRENGTH

> *"Do not be saddened this day, for rejoicing in the Lord must be your strength."*
>
> NEHEMIAH 8:10

In my vision I saw people holding hands in a circle singing and dancing, facing Jesus who was standing in the middle. "My love, when your focus is on me, your heart will rejoice. For I am the solution to all your problems. I see your future and I know the outcome. I know what is best for you. Focus on doing my will and you will be blessed beyond your imagination. You will have strength to carry out all that I have planned for you to do. For my yoke is easy and my burden is light. Do everything with joy. Do not worry about anything. I will help you always. Be joyful and you will be strengthened."

> *Lord Jesus, you are my strength and my joy. I trust you and know that you will be with me today and every day of my life.*

REFLECTION: Is Jesus my strength and my joy in everything I do?

PREACHING THE FAITH

"The one who once was persecuting us is now
preaching the faith he once tried to destroy."

GALATIANS 1:23

In my vision I saw Paul preaching to people in the marketplace. "My child, there are many ways to share your faith with others. The important thing is to go out and do it. Let people know how blessed they are because they are children of God. Their life here on earth has meaning and purpose. You are called to share your conversion story with them. You will be filled with joy when you preach the good news and build my kingdom. When people see how blessed you are, they will want to have what you have. They will be eager to listen to you. Be brave and be bold like Paul."

My Jesus, give me the courage to step out of my
comfort zone to share your gospel with others.
May you be glorified and praised forever.

REFLECTION: Do I share my conversion stories and share my faith with others?

DAILY BREAD

*"Give us each day our daily bread
and forgive us our sins."*

LUKE 11:3-4

In my vision I saw Jesus sitting with his disciples at the last supper. He blessed the bread and gave it to them to eat. "My beloved, you need nourishment and food for your journey here on earth. Therefore the night before I was to suffer I instituted the Eucharist – which is my body and blood. I gave you myself to be consumed by all my disciples. Whoever eats my body and drinks my blood will have eternal life. For my body is true food and my blood is true drink that will nourish you each day. I will give you love, peace and joy when you are in communion with me. I am your bread of life."

*Thank you, Jesus, for giving us your most
precious body and blood each day. My
soul hungers and thirsts for you.*

REFLECTION: How often do I receive the body and the blood of Jesus, who is the bread of life?

PRAYER AND PETITION

"Have no anxiety at all, but in everything,
by prayer and petition, with thanksgiving,
make your requests known to God."

PHILIPPIANS 4:6

In my vision I saw myself sitting on a lounge chair at a beautiful beach with deep blue sky above me and a turquoise ocean in front of me. "My precious one, with me at your side you have no need to worry nor feel anxious. For I have you in the palms of my hands. Rest in me and trust in me. All will be well. If you have any need or problems to solve, just pray about it and I will help you to resolve everything. Do not feel that you are ever alone, but feel confident that I will always be ready to answer all your prayers and petitions. Have I refused you anything yet?"

No, my Lord Jesus. You have always answered
all my prayers and petitions. I am so grateful
for your love and care. Thank you, Jesus.

REFLECTION: Do I pray and give thanks to Jesus, who is always by my side?

WELCOMED HIM

*"Jesus entered a village where a woman
whose name was Martha welcomed him."*

LUKE 10:38

In my vision I saw a little child who was looking out the window waiting for his father to come home. When he finally came back from work, the child was jumping with joy and leaped into his arms. "My loving child, be a lookout for me always. Be ready for me any minute. Wait with love and patience in your heart. Keep watching and staying alert for I will be coming soon. Do not get weary, but keep yourself busy with good works. Prepare your heart to receive me and to welcome me with open arms. I am coming when you least expect me."

*Loving Jesus, I long for the day when I
can welcome you into my arms. I will
wait patiently to be with you forever.*

REFLECTION: Am I ready to welcome Jesus into my heart and be a guest in my home?

HEAR THE WORD

"Blessed are those who hear the word of God and observe it."

LUKE 11:28

In my vision I saw Mary was sitting at Jesus' feet and listening attentively to his teaching. "My love, take time out of your busy life and sit quietly alone with me. I long to spend quality time alone with you. Only in this way your love for me will grow. You will know my will and my deepest desires for you. Listen with love and you will be transformed into my way of thinking and doing things. Through listening you will learn what is really important in this life and what is not. Put everything you have learned into practice and you will be blessed abundantly."

Speak, Lord, I am listening. My deepest desire is to live each day to be pleasing to you and to do your will.

REFLECTION: When is the best time for me to sit quietly alone with Jesus and listen to him?

SUN OF JUSTICE

> *"But for you who fear my name, there will arise the sun of justice with its healing rays."*
>
> MALACHI 3:20

In my vision I saw Jesus with rays coming out of his divine heart and hands. "My child, do not be afraid of the last judgement. For I am a God of mercy and compassion. I came to redeem you and to save you. Be mindful of my commandments and my decrees and you will have nothing to worry about. For you have lived a life of purity and honesty. You have tried to live each day with kindness and obedience. Your name is already written in the book of life. I have you carved in my heart. Every day you tried your best to follow my instructions. Now come into my kingdom."

> *Loving Jesus, pour your healing rays upon me so that I may be saved. Thank you for all your love and compassion for me.*

REFLECTION: Do I believe that Jesus will be merciful and loving towards me at the last judgement?

HOW YOU LIVE

*"Watch carefully then how you live,
not as foolish persons but as wise."*

EPHESIANS 5:15

In my vision I saw a young girl with a basket and she was giving bread to the poor. "My beloved, the more generous you are with others, the happier you will be. Always be thoughtful of other people's needs. This way you are imitating me. You will be filled with joy and peace when you are caring for another. You are created to be a helper and a giver. The more you give the more you will receive. Choose to live an abundant life by giving your time, talents and your money to all those who are in need. Be mindful of others and they will be forever grateful to you. You will be blessed abundantly."

O Jesus, thank you for being so kind and generous with me. Help me to be more mindful of other people's needs and to help them to grow closer to you, Lord.

REFLECTION: Am I a helper and a generous giver toward everyone who is less fortunate than I am?

ASK

> *"I tell you, ask and you will receive;*
> *seek and you will find; knock and*
> *the door will be opened to you."*
>
> LUKE 11:9

In my vision I saw Jesus kneeling and praying to his Father. "My precious child, I hear you every time when you pray in my name, because I love you and care about you deeply. I will give you whatever you ask from me if it is good for you. My answer is always "Yes." When you don't get what you want, it may be because the timing is not right. I know when it is the best time for you to receive what you have asked for. If my answer is not what you have in mind, it is because I am giving you something better than what you have asked me. Trust in me with your whole heart and have faith in me."

> *My loving Jesus, I do trust you and*
> *know that you always hear me. Thank*
> *you for answering all my prayers.*

REFLECTION: Do I believe that Jesus will always give me what I ask from him?

BAPTIZED INTO CHRIST

"For through faith you are all children of God in Christ Jesus. For all of you who were baptized into Christ have clothed yourself with Christ."

GALATIANS 3:26-27

In my vision I saw a little girl dressed all in white ready to be baptized. She was beaming with pride and joy. "My child, when you are clothed in Christ, all your actions will imitate those of Christ. You will speak with love and gentleness. Your eyes will see those who are less fortunate than yourself. Your heart will go out to all who need your help. You will walk in my light and bring good tidings to all who need to hear them. You will have compassion for the broken-hearted and be more generous in all you do for others. In other words, imitate me and be Christ to others."

Lord Jesus, let me be like you in everything I do and say. Let your love and light shine upon all those who come into my life.

REFLECTION: Do I try to imitate Christ in every action I do each day?

COMPASSION

> *"I will have compassion on them, as a man*
> *has compassion on his son who serves him."*
>
> MALACHI 3:17

In my vision I saw a servant washing someone's feet. "My beloved, the more you serve others with love, the more you will receive compassion on the day of your judgment. You will be rewarded a hundred fold for every good deed you do for my Father's honor and glory. Love without service is like an empty gong. Many people go to church but their hearts are far from me. They go so that they are seen by their friends. Then on Monday they live their lives like everything for their own glory. Be my servant and my disciple. Only in this way I will have compassion for you as my own son."

> *Jesus, I want to serve you as my Lord*
> *and Savior. Use me in whatever you have*
> *planned for me each day. Fill my heart with*
> *your love and compassion for others.*

REFLECTION: Am I compassionate and willing to serve others as Jesus did for me?

SPIRITUAL BLESSINGS

"Blessed be the God and Father of our Lord Jesus Christ, who has blessed us in Christ with every spiritual blessing in the heavens."

EPHESIANS 1:3

In my vision I saw a glass jar full of colorful round balls like jells for the bubble bath. "My dearest one, the day when you were baptized you were given all the spiritual blessings from heaven. These spiritual blessings will follow you all the days of your life. They are like the colorful round balls you saw in your vision. Each blessing will bless you at different times of your life. Be assured that my blessings always go before you. I will lead you to my Father's house; He will welcome you with open arms and you will be showered with His love and blessing."

Thank you, Lord Jesus, for all what you have done for me. Please continue to pour your blessings upon me and my family.

REFLECTION: Do I realize that Jesus showered me with all his blessings when I was baptized?

YOKE OF SLAVERY

> *"For freedom Christ set us free; so stand firm
> and do not submit again to the yoke of slavery."*
> GALATIANS 5:1

In my vision I saw slaves building the Pyramid. They were suffering from hard work. "My beloved, you are all called to be sons and daughters of God, not to be slave to the ambitions of this world. Do not spend your life chasing after riches and fame. They only lead you to destruction and death. See how many famous people end up overdosed with drugs and die young. I have chosen you to be my children. So from now on do not submit to the yoke of slavery. For I have set you free from all your sins. Stand firm and start storing treasures in heaven instead."

> *My Jesus, set me free from these worldly
> desires. Help me to walk in your ways
> and follow you all the way to heaven.*

REFLECTION: Am I a slave chasing riches in this world or am I willing to be a slave for the love of Jesus?

EYES OF YOUR HEARTS

*"May the eyes of your hearts be
enlightened, that you may know what
is the hope that belongs to his call."*

EPHESIANS 1:18

In my vision I saw a blind man, who after washing in the
pool could finally see. He was leaping and jumping with
joy. "My child, when you see things with your heart it
is different from seeing with your eyes. You will understand a situation from a very different perspective. You
will see things like how I see them. You will be filled
with wisdom and understanding when you see from
your heart. Open your heart always and you will know
my will. For my will is always loving and caring for others. I see your heart and I know what goes on in your
mind. Be opened and be enlightened."

*Open my eyes of the heart, Lord, so that I
may see you clearly in every situation. Fill
me with more wisdom and understanding.*

REFLECTION: Do I see people with my eyes or with
my heart?

GIVE ALMS

> *"As to what is within, give alms, and*
> *behold, everything will be clean for you."*
> LUKE 11:41

In my vision I saw a beggar with withered legs sitting by the sidewalk. "My loving child, when you give alms your heart is moved with pity and mercy for the poor and the helpless. It is your heart that I see. The more generous you are with others, the more my Father will bless you. So give alms with a joyful heart whenever you see a person who is less fortunate than you are. They are helpless without your love and your generosity. The more you give the more treasures you will be storing in heaven. Be at peace and know that all your sins are forgiven."

> *Loving Jesus, thank you for teaching*
> *me to be always ready to give alms and*
> *to help those who are in need.*

REFLECTION: Do I give alms generously with a joyful heart?

LAMBS AMONG WOLVES

"Go on your way, behold, I am sending you like lambs among wolves."

LUKE 10:3

In my vision I saw a tapestry of saints on their way to heaven. Many of them have been martyred. "My beloved, be vigilant always especially when you go out to proclaim my good news to others. The evil one will be there to harm you and to prevent you from carrying out my wishes. So pray constantly. Pray and ask your guardian angel to protect you from all evil. This world is full of wolves who are ready to destroy you. But fear not, I am always with you. Pray with the angels and the saints and ask them to intercede for you. Never go out alone but two by two like my disciples did."

Lord Jesus, you are my rock and my shelter. Come and protect me from all harm. All the angels and saints, please pray for me.

REFLECTION: Do I ask my guardian angel to protect me when I go out to do God's work?

THRONE OF GRACE

*"So let us confidently approach the throne of grace
to receive mercy and to find grace for timely help."*

HEBREWS 4:16

In my vision I saw myself standing in front of a shining throne. The bright light revealed all my sins like black dots on a white garment. From the throne a light beam burned away all my black spots and my garment gradually became as white as snow. "My little one, come before my throne with your repentant heart. Do not try to hide your sins from me so that I can remove them with my mercy and grace. Be honest and surrender yourself to me. I will purify you and transform you into my image and likeness. Come with confidence that my mercy will wash you clean and restore your soul again."

*My Jesus, I come before you in all my
sinfulness. Pour your graces and mercy
upon me and wash me clean again.*

REFLECTION: Am I ready to approach God's throne with confidence that I will receive mercy and grace?

HOLY SPIRIT

*"The Holy Spirit will teach you at that
moment what you should say."*

LUKE 12:12

I saw Jesus being baptized at the River Jordon. A dove
descended upon him and a voice from heaven said, "This
is my beloved son." "My child, at your baptism the Holy
Spirit descended upon you also. From that day on you
are filled with the Spirit. He will guide you every day
if you invite him into your heart. He will whisper in
your ear where you need to go and what to say. He will
prompt you in times of need and encourage you when
you are in trouble. He will open your eyes to see things
clearly. So remember to invite the Holy Spirit to be with
you each day as you go out to do my Father's will."

*Loving Jesus, please send the Holy Spirit
upon me each day so that I will be able
to do your work with his guidance.*

REFLECTION: Have I invited the Holy Spirit to
come into my heart and asked him to teach me?

BY GRACE

*"For by grace you have been saved through faith,
and this is not from you; it is the gift of God;
it is not from works, so no one may boast."*

EPHESIANS 2:8-9

In my vision I saw a person ready to take his shower. At first he was covered with dirt and mud but after the shower he was dressed nice and clean. "My precious one, you have been washed clean by my blood and water. You are saved because of my death on the cross. I have chosen you and have called you by name. Before your baptism you were covered with sin. Now you become my precious child, a child set apart to be holy and pure. From that day on you are mine. I will shower you with my grace and mercy. You have been saved through your faith in me. It is a pure gift from God."

*Thank you, my beloved Jesus, for your
mercy and grace. May you be praised
and adored forever and ever.*

REFLECTION: Do I have faith in Jesus that I have been saved by his grace at my baptism?

PRESENT DAY

> *"You know how to interpret the appearance of the earth and the sky; why do you not know how to interpret the present day?"*
>
> LUKE 12:56

In my vision I saw a weatherman reporting that there will be hurricanes, flooding, storms and extreme weather changes. "My child, many things are happening each day. There will be unrest and persecution all over the world. Be prepared and stand firm in your faith. Do not waste any time in idol gossip, but go out to bring my people back into the church. Anyone who is not with me is against me. There are wolves everywhere ready to devour my poor lambs who are lost and do not know the way. Pray hard for their conversion and hold on to me and I will carry you through this tribulation."

> *Merciful Jesus, you are my rock, my shelter and my salvation. Have mercy on us and on the whole world.*

REFLECTION: Am I prepared to face unrest and persecution all over the world at the present day?

CHOSEN

> *"Blessed is the nation whose God is the Lord,*
> *the people chosen as his inheritance."*
>
> PSALM 33:12

In my vision I saw Mary when she was a child and was brought to the temple where she was consecrated to the Lord. "My beloved, you too are chosen and consecrated to me the day you entered the church. You did not choose me but I have chosen you the minute you were conceived in your mother's womb. I love everything about you. You are unique and one of a kind. I know you inside out and have counted every hair on your head. You are precious in my sight. I treasure you more than silver and gold. You are blessed beyond your imagination. So be glad that you are chosen by God."

I am forever grateful to you for choosing me to be your child. I feel so blessed and loved by you, Lord.

REFLECTION: Do I feel blessed and loved for being chosen by God?

GIFT OF GOD

"For the wages of sin is death, but the gift of God is eternal life in Christ Jesus our Lord."

ROMANS 6:23

In my vision I saw a mother who has just given birth to a new baby. She held the child with such loving care. "My precious, your life is a gift from God. Treasure it and nourish it with my word. Everyone who listens to my word and obeys it will have eternal life. Those who choose to go their own way and live a life style contrary to my teaching will surely die. For the wages of sin is death. My child, if you see someone who is going down the wrong path would you not try to help them turn around? People do not realize how precious life is until they are about to lose it. Treasure your gift of eternal life."

Thank you, Jesus, for my life. Everything I have belongs to you. Teach me to live each day for your glory, Lord.

REFLECTION: Do I treasure my life as a gift from God and try to live each day for His glory?

BE SUBORDINATE

*"Be subordinate to one another
out of reverence for Christ."*

EPHESIANS 5:21

In my vision I saw a child listening attentively and obeying his parents at home. "My beloved child, when I was on earth I only did what my Father told me to do, even suffering a most painful death on the cross. You too must live each day in obedience to my Father and ask Him before you step out to do His will. Only subordinating your will to His will produce much fruit. For God loves a humble and submissive heart. Be obedient to those who are superior and older than yourself. Always think highly of others. Only in this way you can be my true disciple."

*Make my heart humble and meek, Lord.
Help me to be subordinate to all those
who need my respect and obedience.*

REFLECTION: Do I have a humble and submissive heart and always think highly of others?

SOME ARE LAST

"For behold, some are last who will be first,
and some are first who will be last."

LUKE 13:30

In my vision I saw a group of handicapped children having a race. Some were laughing and holding each other's hands. "My child, no one is perfect in this world. Do not ridicule those who are not as smart or capable as yourself. They are just as precious to me as you are. In fact I see each person's heart and you see only their outward appearances. Those who are least important in the world are just as precious to me as those who are the leaders. Their innocence, loving and compassionate heart are more pleasing to me than those who are proud and self-sufficient. Be humble and be grateful."

Lord, please forgive me for the times
when I was proud and not loving to those
who are less capable than I am.

REFLECTION: Do I realize that the last shall be first in the eyes of Jesus?

REPENT

> *"But I tell you, if you do not repent,*
> *you will all perish as they did!"*
>
> LUKE 13:3

In my vision I saw myself offering my sinful heart to Jesus. He cleaned it with his living water and filled it up with his own blood. "My beloved child, every time when you repent I will wash you clean and will fill your heart with my love. Repentance is necessary for your salvation. For I have given you free will to choose me or to continue to live in the condition that you are in. I will never force myself into your heart. It must be freely offered by you. I will change your heart of stone into a heart of flesh. You can begin anew if you confess your sins and you will not perish but live."

> *Most sacred heart of Jesus, I love you*
> *and I adore you. Please forgive me all the*
> *times when I have sinned against you.*

REFLECTION: Have a confessed all my sins and repented of my sinfulness to Jesus?

BE DOERS

"Be doers of the word and not hearers
only, deluding yourselves."

JAMES 1:22

In my vision I saw people busy carrying heavy stones to build the temple. "My child, everyone is called to build my kingdom. But many people are busy tearing it down with complaints and criticism. Those who are only interested in talking and not working are not my disciples. For my sheep hear my voice and will follow me. They do not follow their own desires. Those who are constantly dissatisfied with the world spend more time tearing it down and not enough time building up my kingdom. Choose wisely. Be doers of my will and you will be blessed abundantly."

Lord Jesus, I only want to do your will.
Help me to choose wisely in all I do each
day to build up your kingdom.

REFLECTION: Do I spend more time complaining and criticizing others instead of building them up?

CHILDREN OF LIGHT

"For you were once darkness, but now you are light in the Lord. Live as children of light."

EPHESIANS 5:8

In my vision I saw Adam and Eve enjoying themselves in the garden. But after they ate the forbidden fruit they were in shame and in darkness. "My beloved, live each day imitating me. This way you will be my children of light. For I am the Light of the World. Anyone who stays close to me and follows me will be filled with my light. You will never be in the darkness if you obey my law and my commandments. You will be free as Adam and Eve before their fall. You will enjoy all the fruits and blessings from me. So be with me always and you will be my children of light."

My Jesus, you are my light and my salvation. In you I trust and adore. I want to follow you always.

REFLECTION: Do I try to live each day as a child of light in the eyes of Jesus?

ARMOR OF GOD

"Put on the armor of God that you may be able to resist on the evil day."

EPHESIANS 6:13

In my vision I saw Joan of Arc in full armor riding a white horse. "My faithful child, the evil one roams around the world like a roaring lion. Be always ready to confront him. Be protected with the armor of God, which is the truth, righteousness, peace, faith and the sword of the Spirit, which is the word of God. Memorize my words so that you can speak them when you are under attack. My words have power and will overcome all evil. In times of temptation, recite my words and call on my name. Only in this way you will be protected from all harm."

Thank you, Lord Jesus, for your words of wisdom. I will put on the armor of God and call on your name in time of trouble.

REFLECTION: Do I put on the armor of God every morning so that I will be protected from harm at all times?

THIRSTY

"All you who are thirsty, come to the water!"

ISAIAH 55:1

In my vision I saw myself kneeling down and drinking water from a crystal clear stream. "My child, I am thirsty for you as you are for the water. Without water you cannot survive. Without me your soul will wither. I am your life and your strength. I will refresh and renew you every time when you come to me. Drink deeply. Fill yourself up with my love and my grace. I am your living water that will supply all your needs. Surrender yourself to me wholeheartedly. Trust in me and I will purify you and refresh you. Come to the water often and drink from me."

My most loving Jesus, you are my living water.
My soul thirsts for you day and night.

REFLECTION: Do I thirst for Jesus as much as I thirst for water?

NOVEMBER

WHITE ROBES

> "They stood before the throne and before
> the Lamb, wearing white robes and
> holding palm branches in their hands."
>
> REVELATION 7:9

In my vision I saw myself dressed in a white robe standing in front of the throne. To my left and right there were a multitude of people from all nations also wearing white robes adoring Jesus. "My loving child, one day you will be in my Father's house and see me face to face. When that day comes you will be filled with joy. All the people around you will welcome you and love you. They will rejoice that you have finished the race and have kept the faith. You have persevered throughout all your trials and tribulations. Well done, my faithful servant. Come and sit with me at my banquet."

> *Lord Jesus, thank you for this beautiful vision*
> *and for your love and assurance. I look forward*
> *to that day when I will be with you for eternity.*

REFLECTION: Can I imagine the joy that I will experience when I will be seeing Jesus face to face?

NEWNESS OF LIFE

> *"We were indeed buried with him through baptism into death, so that, just as Christ was raised from the dead by the glory of the Father, we too might live in newness of life."*
>
> ROMANS 6:4

In my vision I saw myself wearing a new garment smiling and admiring myself in front of a mirror. "My child, when I raise you from the dead you shall surely be wearing a new garment. Everything old will pass away, but my love for you will be with you forever. You will be dressed like a bride ready to meet the groom. Your heart will rejoice and will be filled with love. There will be no more sorrow and regrets. Only joy in the Lord. You will be treasured in heaven beyond your imagination. So love one another as I have loved you. Let your heart sing with joy."

I can hardly wait until I have a new life with you forever in heaven. You are truly my Lord and my God.

REFLECTION: Do I look forward to the day when I will be wearing a new garment and enjoying a new life in heaven?

MORE JOY

> *"There will be more joy in heaven over one sinner who repents than over ninety-nine righteous people who have no need of repentance."*
>
> LUKE 15:7

In my vision I saw a "Welcome Home" sign with balloons in a living room celebrating a lost child coming back home. "My beloved, every time that you repent and confess your sins, the angels in heaven are overjoyed. For your soul and your salvation mean a lot to me and to my Father. Every soul is precious in our sight. When you repent from your old sinful ways, you are set free and will be able to live joyfully in my kingdom. Sin cripples people. Sin separates you from us and from others. Selfishness and self-centeredness leads you away from heaven. So repent and be transformed."

> *Jesus, please forgive me for all the times when I have sinned against you and others. I choose to repent and ask for your forgiveness. Fill me with joy again.*

REFLECTION: Have I repented for my sins so that one day I will be able to live joyfully in heaven with Jesus?

SAME ATTITUDE

*"Have among yourselves the same attitude
that is also yours in Christ Jesus."*

PHILIPPIANS 2:5

In my vision I saw Jesus walking with his disciples and a large crowd of people and children came running towards him. Many of them wanted to touch him. "My little one, when you love people, they will want to be around you. They are energized by your presence. When you speak with people keep your eyes focused on them and speak from your heart. Treat them as you would treat me. Love them as I have loved you. Every person is precious and irreplaceable. Treasure everyone who comes near you for they are all my beloved children."

*Thank you, Jesus, for teaching me how to love
others. Help me to have the same attitude
towards everyone as you have for them.*

REFLECTION: Do I treasure everyone who comes into my life and have the same attitude as Jesus?

STRENGTH FOR EVERYTHING

"I have the strength for everything through him who empowers me."

PHILIPPIANS 4:13

In my vision I saw a person lifting weights and another person running on a stationary treadmill. "My faithful one, if you want to have spiritual strength you need to study my word and pray constantly. For my word has power and when you speak my word you will be empowered. Your strength depends on me. Without me you can do nothing to please my Father. With me you will be able to move mountains. I am your strength and your power. Stay close to me and call on me often. Only in this way you will have the strength and power to make a difference in this world."

My Jesus, you are my rock and my strength. With you I can do all things for your honor and glory, Lord.

REFLECTION: Am I empowered by the word of God and have the strength to make a difference in this world?

DIRCT YOUR HEARTS

"May the Lord direct your hearts to the love
of God and to the endurance of Christ."

2 THESSALONIANS 3:5

In my vision I saw a person aiming an arrow from his archery to the center of the circles on a board. "My child, keep your mind focused on me. If you want to enter my kingdom you should keep your eyes and heart aiming at me and not on earthly pleasures. They distract you from doing the right things here on earth. Keep your eyes focused on my cross and you will see the true meaning and purpose of your life. When your eyes and heart start to wander around, you will miss the mark. Direct your heart on my love for you and you will be saved."

Thank you, Lord, for this revelation. Help me
to always desire you above all things and keep
my mind and heart focused on you only.

REFLECTION: Is my heart focused on Jesus' love for me instead of earthly pleasures?

MY DISCIPLE

> *"Whoever does not carry his own cross and*
> *come after me cannot be my disciple."*
>
> LUKE 14:27

In my vision I saw Jesus carrying a big wooden cross and I was following him with a little cross. "My faithful one, I will never give you more than you can carry. So be not afraid that you will not be strong enough to carry your cross. If you follow me closely you will succeed, like a skier who is just beginning to learn how to ski. If he follows the same path where his teacher is going he will soon learn how to make every turn smoothly and go down the hill safely. So it is in your life. If you imitate me all that I do, you will live each day with peace and joy even during your trials and suffering."

> *Lord Jesus, I want to be your disciple.*
> *With you by my side I will have the*
> *courage to carry my cross to the end.*

REFLECTION: Am I ready to be Jesus' disciple by picking up my cross daily and following him?

GOD KNOWS YOUR HEART

"You justify yourselves in the sight of others, but God knows your hearts; for what is of human esteem is an abomination in the sight of God."

LUKE 16:15

In my vision I saw myself standing in front of an X-ray machine. "My beloved child, I know everything about you. I know you better than you know yourself, because I know what you are thinking and I see your heart and know how you feel. Do not do things so others think better of you. Do things only to please me. Your reward is greater when no one else knows and sees your action. For then I know that you are doing it just for me. Human beings will praise you one day and curse you the next day. But I will always love you and cherish you forever. My love for you is eternal."

My loving Jesus, you know me when I am asleep and when I am awake. Let all my actions be pleasing to you and let my heart be pure and sincere.

REFLECTION: Are all my actions done to please God instead of trying to be justified in the sight of others?

TEMPLE OF GOD

> *"If anyone destroys God's temple, God will destroy that person; for the temple of God, which you are, is holy."*
>
> 1 CORINTHIANS 3:17

In my vision I saw a beautiful temple with water flowing out of it. Everywhere the water flowed, the trees had green leaves and the flowers bloomed. "My child, your body is my beautiful temple. You are created in my image and likeness. Therefore everyone is holy. You must take good care of your body. Let no one destroy another person's body no matter how old or young he is. I am the author of all life. I am the one who can decide when your life will end in this world. No one can decide for themselves when to be born and when to die. Every human being is holy and precious to me."

> *Thank you, God, for giving me life. Help me to take care of my body and to live each day for your honor and glory, Lord.*

REFLECTION: Do I realize that my body is the temple of God and precious in His sight?

SIGHT TO THE BLIND

> *"The Lord gives sight to the blind. The Lord raises up those who were bowed down. The Lord loves the righteous."*
>
> PSALM 146:8

In my vision I saw a blind beggar sitting on his mat as Jesus was passing by. He called out to Jesus to heal him. "My beloved child, many people who can see are actually blind to the spiritual world. They look but do not see. They hear but do not understand. Those who are humble and ask me to restore their sight will be given spiritual eyes to see and ears to hear. Be vigilant and keep your eyes open and you will see signs. Have no fear but have faith in me. Have courage and do not be afraid to step out and to proclaim the good news to others."

> *My Jesus, heal me of my blindness and open my eyes so that I will see you wherever I go. Help me to lead others closer to you.*

REFLECTION: Am I vigilant with my eyes open so that I can see Jesus better?

OUR STRUGGLE

> *"Our struggle is not with flesh and blood but*
> *with the principalities, with the powers, with*
> *the world rulers of this present darkness,*
> *with the evil spirits in the heavens."*
>
> EPHESIANS 6:12

In my vision I saw an exorcist praying with a person holding a crucifix trying to expel the evil spirits from him. "My child, only through prayer and fasting will you be able to conquer the evil one. Do not hate your enemies but love them and pray for their conversion. For your battle is against demons and devils that are within them. Cast them out by your love and fervent prayer. This is a spiritual battle. All things are possible when you ask for my help. Pray constantly for your enemies. Have faith and total trust in me. Call on my name and the evil one will flee."

> *Thank you, Jesus, for giving me the*
> *courage to overcome all evil. Stay with me*
> *always and protect me from all harm.*

REFLECTION: How often do I pray and fast to overcome the evil one?

MUSTARD SEED

"If you have faith the size of a mustard seed, you would say to this mulberry tree, 'Be uprooted and planted in the sea, and it would obey you.'"

LUKE 17:6

In my vision I saw Jesus calming the storm with his spoken word. "My precious child, do your believe that I can stop a storm or walk on water? Nothing is impossible for me. Your words have power too. When you speak them with faith you too can uproot a mulberry tree. Have faith in me and not on your own understanding. With me everything is possible. With me you can move mountains and change this world. So have faith in me and I will do mighty deeds with your cooperation. Ask, you shall receive. Seek, you shall find and knock, it shall be opened."

Lord Jesus, increase my faith in your mighty power. Help me to trust you with all my heart and soul.

REFLECTION: Do I have faith in Jesus and believe that all things are possible with him?

MY WORDS

"Desire therefore my words; long for them and you shall be instructed."

WISDOM 6:11

In my vision I saw a hand writing words on the wall. "My beloved, my words have power and can change hearts. My words can heal and mold people's minds. My words are the truth and the truth will set you free. Knowing my words will give you life and joy. Memorize my words in the scripture and you will have wisdom and power to transform this world. It is through my words that I have created you and the entire universe. Nothing happens without my words. Study my words and meditate them day and night. They are more precious than gold or silver."

Thank you for your everlasting words, Jesus. Without them I am lost, because your words are a lamp to my feet and they guide me in everything I do each day.

REFLECTION: Do I study and memorize the words in the scripture day and night?

IMPERISHABLE

"God formed us to be imperishable; in the image of his own nature he made us."

WISDOM 2:23

In my vision I saw Adam and Eve eating the forbidden fruit that the devil enticed them to eat. "My child, if you follow my commandments you will live forever in heaven with me. The reason Adam and Eve were sent out of the Garden of Eden is that they have disobeyed me. I came into this world to save you by my obedience to my Father. I died on the cross for all your sins so that you will live forever. For I love you and never want to be separated from you. Avoid evil at all cost and live each day following my word and my commandments. Only in this way you will be assured eternal life in heaven."

Lord Jesus, I will try my best to be obedient to all your commandments and follow your words all the days of my life. I want to spend eternity with you in heaven.

REFLECTION: Do I realize that I am imperishable and will live forever if I follow God's commandments daily?

GIVE THANKS

> *"'Has none but this foreigner returned to give*
> *thanks to God?' Then he said to him, 'Stand*
> *up and go;, your faith has saved you.'"*
>
> LUKE 17:18-19

In my vision I saw a leper who was healed kneeling in front of Jesus and thanking him profusely. "My child, everyone who came to me for healing was healed. But only a few came back to thank me. Those who are grateful for their healing were saved because they believed that I am the Son of the living God. Many of them came after me and became my disciples. They realized that I am their Messiah and their Savior. If you truly believe in me you will also be saved and have everlasting life. Have faith in me with a thankful and grateful heart and you will blessed with an abundant life."

> *My Jesus and my savior, I thank you and*
> *praise you for all that you have done for*
> *me. I am forever grateful for your love.*

REFLECTION: Am I thankful and grateful to God for giving me an abundant life?

ANTICHRIST

> *"Many deceivers have gone out into the word, those who do not acknowledge Jesus Christ as coming in the flesh; such is the deceitful one and the antichrist."*
>
> 2 JOHN 1:7

In my vision I saw Hitler giving a speech in front of a mob of people, all holding flags in their hands waving them with excitement. "My beloved, do not be deceived by false leaders and prophets. Their promises will only end with destruction, suffering and war. Anyone who does not believe in me is against me. They are your enemies. They come to deceive you with false hope. Be alert and be wise. Do not follow anyone who is disobedient to my commandments. They will only lead you to hopelessness and despair. They are the antichrist. Come and follow me."

> *Protect me from the deceivers, O Lord.*
> *Be with me always so that I will only*
> *walk with you and follow you.*

REFLECTION: Do I realize that there are many deceivers and antichrists in this world?

PRAY ALWAYS

> *"Jesus told his disciples a parable*
> *about the necessity for them to pray*
> *always without becoming weary."*
>
> LUKE 18:1

In my vision I saw Jesus praying alone early in the morning. "My faithful one, the only way to know what is my Father's will for you is to spend time alone with Him every day. He will reveal to you the path you must go. He will show you what you need to do in each situation. He will give you the right words to say and how to deal with others with love. Prayer is your lifeline to heaven. That is why I spend each morning alone with my Father. He will give you the strength to live each day with courage and to face each trial with peace in your heart. Pray always and pray without ceasing."

> *I praise you and I thank you for always*
> *being there for me, Lord. Thank you*
> *for answering all my prayers.*

REFLECTION: Do I spend time alone with Jesus and pray for his guidance every day?

THE WISE

"The wise shall shine brightly like the splendor of the firmament, and those who lead the many to justice shall be like the stars forever."

DANIEL 12:3

In my vision I saw that the five wise bridesmaids with their lanterns went to meet the groom when he arrived. "My dear child, be wise and be prepared to meet me every day. Do not spend your days worrying about what to eat and what to wear. But spend each day loving and praising God. Prepare your heart to receive me when I come. Be not afraid but be vigilant. Let each day be a fruitful day by doing good to others and by sharing what you have with those who are less fortunate. Only in this way you will be ready to enter into my kingdom. Be kind and loving to everyone and you will shine like a star in heaven."

Loving Jesus, you are my bridegroom and my redeemer. I look forward to the day when I will be united with you in heaven.

REFLECTION: Am I living a fruitful life by doing good and sharing what I have with others?

REPROVE AND CHASTISE

"Those whom I love, I reprove and chastise.
Be earnest, therefore, and repent."

REVELATION 3:19

In my vision I saw a child standing in front of his father who was disciplining him. "My child, every parent wants the best for their children. That is why they often discipline and teach them when they do wrong. So does my Father in heaven. He will reprove and chastise you when you are off the track. He knows what you are thinking and will help you to return to him. When you find yourself moving away from him you must turn yourself around and change your ways and repent. For your Father is always ready to welcome you back into his warm embrace."

Father, Son and the Holy Spirit, please forgive
me all the times that I have sinned against you.
Help me to live a holy and righteous life.

REFLECTION: Have I been reproved and chastised by God and finally repented for my wrong doing?

OPENS THE DOOR

*"If anyone hears my voice and opens
the door, then I will enter his house and
dine with him, and he with me."*

REVELATIONS 3:20

In my vision I heard someone knocking at my door.
When I opened it I saw Jesus standing there. "My precious, I am always knocking at your heart for I love you
with an everlasting love and want to be with you forever.
Open your heart to receive me and I will never leave you
nor forsake you. For you are mine and I treasure every
moment we spend together. Invite me to dwell within
you throughout the day and spend time alone with me.
Those moments are more precious than anything you
can do to please me. Your love is what I desire most. I
thirst for you."

*I love you, Jesus, with all my heart and
soul. Please come and dwell within me. Let
me never be separated away from you.*

REFLECTION: Am I ready to open my heart and
invite Jesus to dine with me?

HOUSE OF PRAYER

> *"My house shall be a house of prayer, but*
> *you have made it a den of thieves."*
>
> LUKE 19:46

In my vision I saw a person praying in a beautiful cathedral like Notre Dame. "My child, if you want me to dwell in you, you must put me first in your life. Many people do not realize that they spend more hours worrying about money than praying to me. They make every decision according to how much it will cost them. My love, you know that I will provide for all your needs. Do you really trust me 100%? If you do, then you will be praising and thanking me every day. You will turn your heart into a house of prayer. Focus on me and you will have everything your heart desires."

> *Come Lord Jesus, live in my mind, dwell in*
> *my heart, and be the center moment of my*
> *life. You alone will I worship and adore.*

REFLECTION: How much time do I spend worrying about money instead of praising and thanking Jesus?

THE LORD IS KING

*"The Lord is king, in splendor robed; robed
in the Lord and girt about with strength."*

PSALM 93:1

In my vision I saw Jesus' face imprinted on Veronica's
cloth with marks of thorns on his head and his face
covered with blood. "My beloved child, do not feel pity
on my suffering, but rejoice. For I came to redeem you
from all your inequities. You are set free from all your
sins. Come and be my disciple, always ready to go out
and proclaim the good news to everyone. One day you
will join me in my kingdom. For I have set you free by
my cross. I am the King of kings and the Lord of lords.
Sing praise and rejoice with me with thanksgiving and
a grateful heart."

*Jesus, I praise you and I adore you, my
King and my Lord. You are my savior and
my redeemer. You alone will I serve.*

REFLECTION: Do I believe that Jesus has redeemed
me from all my inequities?

YOU MUST PROPHESY

*"You must prophesy again about many
people, nations, tongues and kings."*

REVELATION 10:11

In my vision I saw Paul preaching and teaching to everyone who was there to listen to him. "My faithful one, you too are called to prophesy, teach and preach to others. I have given you the gift to share your stories to all who to need hear them. You are my mouth and my hands now. Go and lay hands on my people. Pray for healing and blessings upon them and share your prophesy with them so that they too will believe in me. Do not be afraid to proclaim all that I have done for you and share your joy with them. You will be blessed a hundred fold in heaven."

*Thank you, my precious Jesus, for giving me the
courage to go and proclaim the good news and
prophesy to everyone who is willing to listen.*

REFLECTION: Do I realize that I am called by Jesus to prophesy, teach and preach?

INNER SELF

> *"We are not discouraged; rather, although our outer self is wasting away, our inner self is being renewed day by day."*
>
> 2 CORINTHIANS 4:16

In my vision I was opening a set of Russian lacquered dolls from outside in. "My child, let your inner beauty shine through. Do not worry about your outer appearance. For everyone will grow old one day. Be concerned with your inner self which will shine forever. I see your heart and I am more concerned about your soul which will live forever. For your body will die one day, but your soul will never perish. Keep your heart pure and holy. Let it never be tarnished by evil desires and impure thoughts. Let your heart be filled with my love and grace."

> *Change my inner self to your image and likeness, Lord. Renew my heart with your compassionate love and grace.*

REFLECTION: Am I concerned about my inner self and do I try to live a pure and holy life?

WARS AND INSURRECTIONS

> "When you hear of wars and insurrections, do
> not be terrified; for such things must happen
> first, but it will not immediately be the end."
>
> LUKE 21:9

In my vision I saw airplanes dropping bombs and people frantically running to find shelter. "My little one, there will be many wars and insurrections before the end will be here. The tribulation will follow. There will be earthquakes and famine. Be not afraid. I will be with you through it all. Stay close to me and I will protect you from all harm. Pray constantly and listen to my guidance. I will tell you where to go and what to do. You will be safe with me. Be prepared to act when I tell you. I will bring you to safety. Remember you are my precious child. I will never forsake you nor leave you."

> All loving and compassionate Jesus, give
> me the courage to overcome all fear and
> to stay faithful to you till the end.

REFLECTION: Do I trust Jesus that he will protect me from all harm especially during wars and insurrections?

PARADISE

> *"Amen, I say to you, today you will be with me in paradise."*
>
> LUKE 23:43

In my vision I saw a beautiful garden with large trees bearing fruits like apples and pears. "My beloved, yes I have prepared a place for you where you will never lack of anything. Everything surrounding you will be a feast for your eyes. There will be butterflies and birds singing. You will feel welcomed and loved by everyone. You will see beauty everywhere you go. Nothing will take away your peace and joy in this paradise. You will feast on sumptuous food and the best of wine. There will be no more tears, sorrow and pain, but total bliss. Stay close to me and I will lead you there one day."

Yes, Lord, I look forward to the day when I will be with you for eternity. You are all I want and need.

REFLECTION: Am I prepared and ready to spend eternity with Jesus in paradise?

HE NOTICED

"When Jesus looked up he saw some wealthy people putting their offerings into the treasury and he noticed a poor widow putting in two small coins."

LUKE 21:1-2

In my vision Jesus was looking into my heart. "My child, I know you inside out. I notice your every deed and every thought. Do not judge others because you do not know what is in their minds and hearts. All you see is their outward action, which may be misleading. Some actions seem to be holy and yet they might be done for show. Some deeds may not seem too good and yet they might be done with great love. Let me do the judging. No matter how small a sacrifice you make for me I will notice it and will reward you greatly. Be pure of heart and do not compare yourself with others."

Help me to do everything with great love for your honor and glory, Lord, and remind me never to judge others.

REFLECTION: Am I aware that Jesus notices everything I do and every thought in my mind?

LORD'S GLORY

"For over all, the Lord's glory will be shelter
and protection: shade from the parching heat
of the day and cover from storm and rain."

ISAIAH 4:6

In my vision I saw a double rainbow in the sky with all different colors. "My precious one, it is my promise to you that I will always protect you and be with you wherever you go. You can count on me. It is my nature to love you more than you can ever imagine, because I have created you in my image and likeness. I treasure you and only want the best for you. Even though there are storms and rain in your life, you will not be harmed. My loving arms are surrounding you and shielding you from all trials. You can trust in me and have total confidence in me. I will always be your shelter and protection."

My Jesus, you are truly my rock and
my Savior. Whenever I am under the
weather I will remember to always call
on you for your help and protection.

REFLECTION: Is Jesus my shelter and my protection during storms in my life?

HOLY MOUNTAIN

*"There shall be no harm or ruin on all my holy
mountain; for the earth shall be filled with
knowledge of the Lord, as water covers the sea."*

ISAIAH 11:9

In my vision I saw a mountain with the peak rising
above the cloud. "My beloved, come to my holy mountain and celebrate with me the goodness of the Lord.
On the mountain there will be no more tears nor sorrow. Joy and delight will prevail. The peace will reign
from East to West and North to South. There will be no
more war and killing. In their place, the love and mercy
of the Lord will pour out from your heart. Everyone will
be able to enjoy each other's company without quarrel-
ing and fighting. Even the animals will live peacefully
together. Come to my holy mountain and spend eternity with me."

*Thank you, Jesus, for inviting me to dwell
on the holy mountain with you. May
you be praised and glorified forever.*

REFLECTION: Am I ready to join Jesus on the holy
mountain where there will be no more tears nor sorrow?

JESUS IS LORD

> *"If you confess with your mouth that Jesus is Lord and believe in your heart that God raised him from the dead, you will be saved."*
>
> ROMANS 10:9

In my vision I saw a child Jesus dressed in white with a gold crown on his head. In his right hand he held a gold staff and in his left he held a globe all in gold. "My child, I am the Lord of the universe. I came into the world to save you and to bring you home with me. Anyone who believes in me will have eternal life. Open your eyes and see the truth. The truth will set you free. You are no longer a slave to sin but a new creation. For I dwell in your heart and you belong to me. Through me you are saved and inherited everything. Have faith in me."

> *My Lord and my God, I do believe that you are my savior and my redeemer. I adore and worship you with all my heart.*

REFLECTION: Have I confessed that Jesus is Lord and believed that he has come to save me from my sins?

DECEMBER

ETERNAL ROCK

> *"Trust in the Lord forever! For the*
> *Lord is an eternal Rock."*
>
> ISAIAH 26:4

In my vision I saw the Gibraltar Rock sitting magnificently at the Mediterranean Sea. "My faithful child, I am your rock and your salvation. You can count on me. I will forever stand by you and be there for you through thick and thin. I will protect you from all the storms in your life. Nothing will overcome my love for you. Stand firm on your faith in me and I will support you till the end of times. You can lean on me and call on me in times of trouble. I will always be there for you. There is nothing to worry about but hope in my mighty saving power. For I am your eternal Rock."

> *My most merciful and loving Jesus, you*
> *are my rock and my salvation. I know I*
> *can put all my trust and faith in you.*

REFLECTION: Do I turn to Jesus for help when I am in trouble?

EYES WERE OPENED

*"Then he touched their eyes and said,
'Let it be done for you according to your
faith.' And their eyes were opened."*

MATTHEW 9:29-30

In my vision I saw Jesus touching my eyes and suddenly I could see bright light all around me. "My love, many people have eyes but do not see. But I have opened your spiritual eyes because you have faith in me and believe in me. When you see the world with my eyes, you will see how beautiful everything is. Just like when you were driving through your neighborhood during the Christmas time and saw many houses decorated with lights. Everything sparkled! When your spiritual eyes are opened, you will see every soul as I see them and know how special every person is."

*Lord Jesus, open my eyes so that I will
be able to see you and know you better.
You are my healer and my redeemer.*

REFLECTION: Do I see the world with my own eyes or with the eyes of Jesus?

SEVEN BASKET FULL

"They all ate and were satisfied. They picked up the fragments left over seven baskets full."

MATTHEW 15:37

In my vision I saw Peter pulling his net which was full of fish. He was so surprised. "My child, I am a God of abundance. You will never lack of anything. I can multiply whatever you have when you share them with others. You will be as amazed as Peter in your vision. I can multiply a few fish to feed a multitude of people and still have seven baskets full left over. Do you believe me without a doubt? Share what you have with everyone who asks from you. I promise that you will never go hungry. For I am a generous God and only want the best for my children."

O Jesus, you are truly the King of kings and Lord of lords. Enlarge my heart so that I will always be generous with others as you are with me.

REFLECTION: Do I believe that I have a generous God who will provide for all my needs?

LET US REJOICE

"This is the Lord for whom we looked; let us rejoice and be glad that he has saved us."

ISAIAH 25:9

In my vision I saw a little child running towards his Daddy with open arms ready to be picked up. "My little one, do you look forward to my coming? Do you run to me with your open arms? I am always ready to receive you into my open arms. I will carry you like a loving father and protect you from all harm. You can tell me all that is in your heart. I love to hear every detail of your daily life. Nothing is a waste of time when you are with me. I will listen with joy and compassion when you come to me. I treasure every moment that we spend together. Look for me and you will be filled with joy."

Loving Jesus, my heart rejoices when I am with you. I can hardly wait for the day when I will see you face to face.

REFLECTION: Have I spent time alone with Jesus and conversed with him heart to heart?

RANSOMED

"Those whom the Lord has ransomed
will return and enter Zion singing,
crowned with everlasting joy."

ISAIAH 35:10

In my vision I saw a little lamb being sacrificed at the altar in a temple. But Jesus came and untied it and set the lamb free. "My beloved, I am the Lamb of God. I have died on the cross for all your sins. If you believe in me and profess on your lips that I am your Lord and Savior, you will be ransomed with my blood. You are mine and nothing can snatch you away from me. One day you will enter heaven and sing praises with joy. That day is coming. Keep your soul clean and follow my commandments. You will be saved and live with me forever in heaven."

Thank you, my precious Jesus, for dying
on the cross for me so that I am set free
and will be with you for eternity.

REFLECTION: Do I look forward to the day when I will join Jesus in heaven with joy?

GIVE COMFORT

> *"Comfort, give comfort to my people, says
> your God. Speak tenderly to Jerusalem, and
> proclaim to her that her service is at an end."*
>
> ISAIAH 40:1-2

In my vision I saw a person sick in bed. A nurse was
standing next to him ministering to him with tenderness
and kind words. "My faithful one, people are hurting and
need to hear your comforting words to them. Give them
hope and joy during this Advent season. Bring gifts and
help them in their need. Pray with them and enlighten
their minds and hearts to receive me. For I am the Light
of the World. Anyone who believes in me will be filled
with joy and peace. I came into the world to bring hope
and comfort to everyone. Be my disciple and go out to
proclaim the good news to all."

> *Jesus, Prince of Peace, have mercy on all the poor
> and suffering people. Use me and give me the
> courage to go out and give comfort to everyone.*

REFLECTION: During this advent season am I prepared to go out to bring gifts and hope to those in need?

AMAZED

"The crowds were amazed when they saw the
mute speaking, the deformed made whole,
the lame walked, and the blind able to see,
and they glorified the God of Israel."

MATTHEW 15:31

In my vision I saw people lined up to be prayed over for healing by Jesus. "My child, I came into this world to heal and to save all those who come to me. My heart goes out to them with mercy and compassion. No one goes home empty-handed. Everyone who comes to me will be healed and transformed. So go forth and bring as many people to me as you can. I will heal them and give them words of comfort. I will restore all those who are broken-hearted and lost hope. Spread the good news to everyone who needs healing. I will pour out my blessings upon each one who comes to me during this holy season."

O loving and merciful Jesus, I believe in
your healing power. I praise you and glorify
you for all your amazing miracles.

REFLECTION: Have I brought people closer to Jesus for healing and blessing during this holy season?

MARY

"Do not be afraid, Mary, for you
have found favor with God."

LUKE 1:30

In my vision I saw God the Father crowning Mary in heaven. "My beloved child, you too will receive a crown when you reach heaven if you imitate my mother Mary. She lived every day loving me and caring for me while I was on earth. She sacrificed her own dreams and desires so that she could do my will. She was full of grace and was chosen to be my mother. She was obedient unto death and always merciful and compassionate to everyone. She is your model. Ask her to assist you and to bring you closer to me. She loves you as much as I love you. Her heart and mine beat as one."

Hail Mary, full of grace, pray for me now
and at the hour of my death. Teach me
how to love Jesus as much as you do.

REFLECTION: Is Mary my model on how to love Jesus as much as she did so that one day I too will receive the crown?

LIFE AND DEATH

"Before everyone are life and death,
whichever they choose will be given them."
SIRACH 15:17

In my vision I saw two rooms. In one lighted room a woman was kneeling and praying. In the other room a man was searching for something in the dark. "My child, when you are with me, you are choosing life. For I am the Way, the Truth and the Life. When you spend time praying and listening to me, you will be filled with hope and joy. But, if you choose to do things your way, you are like the man fumbling in the dark who cannot find what he truly wants and desires. It only leads you to frustration and despair. Choose life and live in my light. Only in this way you will be able to see where you are going."

My loving Jesus, I choose you above all else. I want
to live each day for your honor and glory, Lord.

REFLECTION: Am I living a life in the light of Jesus and following his ways instead of my own?

FILLED WITH JOY

> *"Lord has done great things for*
> *us; we are filled with joy."*
> PSALM 126:3

In my vision I saw people all holding hands around a Christmas tree singing a joyful song. "My loving child, let your heart be filled with my joy. The more you are grateful for what I have done for you, the more joyful you will be. A joyful heart is music to my ears. I love to shower blessings upon you and your family. So be grateful every day and know that I will always love you. You have nothing to worry about. I am a generous God and only want to lavish you with all my graces and blessings. Sing praises daily and my peace beyond your understanding will descend upon you."

> *I praise you and thank you for all that you*
> *have done for me, Lord Jesus Christ. I am*
> *forever grateful for your loving care for me.*

REFLECTION: Is my heart filled with gratitude and joy and ready to sing praises to God daily?

RENEW YOUR STRENGTH

> *"They that hope in the Lord will renew their strength, they will soar as the eagle's wings; they will run and not grow weary, walk and not grow faint."*
>
> ISAIAH 40:31

In my vision I saw a person riding a horse with great speed. "My precious child, when you come to me for assistance you will find yourself riding on my strength and my wisdom. Everything will work out easier with my help. You will be amazed how fast and easy the solution will be. It will be less stressful when you put your trust in me. During this Advent, remember to ask me to help you and I will solve all your problems for you. For my yoke is easy and my burden light. Have no ambition on your own. Lean on me and I will give you strength."

Precious Jesus, I surrender myself into your care. I trust you and I know that you will provide the strength I need to do your will each day.

REFLECTION: Do I remember to ask Jesus to strengthen me and to help me to solve all my problems?

SPRINGS OF WATER

> *"I will turn the desert into a marshland, and*
> *the dry ground into springs of water."*
>
> ISAIAH 41:18

In my vision I saw children playing at a fountain that shoots up water from the ground. They were all laughing and jumping with joy. "My child, I am the living water. My well will never run dry. Anyone who comes to me will be like the children in your vision. You will jump with joy knowing that I am with you and there is nothing to worry about. You will have plenty of living water to share with everyone around you. You will dance with laughter if you only know what a treasure you have in your heart. Live in my living water and you will never thirst again."

> *Lord, pour your living water upon me. I want*
> *to be filled with your hope and joy forever so*
> *that I will never be anxious about anything.*

REFLECTION: Am I aware that the living water of Jesus is in my soul and quenching all my thirst?

LIKE A TREE

> *"He is like a tree planted near running*
> *water, that yields its fruit in due season,*
> *and whose leaves never fade."*
>
> PSALM 1:3

In my vision I saw a beautifully decorated Christmas tree with an angel on top and lots of presents below. "My faithful one, be like the Christmas tree in your vision. You will be guided by my angel and my light will shine through you to everyone who is near you. I have given you lots of gifts to give to others who are in need. The more you give the more you will receive. You will not grow weary nor feel burned out. You will have energy and joy to do all that I have planned for you to do. Your leaves will always stay green. For I am with you and I will supply for all your needs."

> *Thank you, Jesus, for always being there for me.*
> *With you I will never lack anything, because*
> *I know you are my hope and my savior.*

REFLECTION: Do I believe that the more I give, the more I will receive?

HUMBLE

"He guides the humble to justice, he teaches the humble his way."

Psalm 25:9

In my vision I saw a woman bending down on her knees and washing Jesus' feet. "My little one, anyone who humbles herself to reach me I will bless abundantly. Therefore do not be afraid to come forth with your requests. I will never send you away empty-handed. Only the humble people are willing to go through the narrow gate. They will be greatly rewarded in heaven. Those who are prideful do not need my guidance. They think that they can do everything on their own. Be humble in all you do and ask for my assistance. Believe in me and trust in me with all your heart."

Most loving Jesus, teach me to be humble and dependent on you. You are my rock and my shelter.

REFLECTION: Am I humble in everything I do and do I remember to ask God for His assistance?

SPEAK NO LIES

"They shall do no wrong and speak no lies; nor shall there be found in their mouths a deceitful tongue."

ZEPHANIAH 3:13

In my vision I saw a snake crawling on a dirt road making hissing sounds with its tongue. "My child, do you know that I am the truth and the way? Anyone who lies is not with me. Because I only speak the truth. The evil one is a deceiver and he likes to distort the truth. Anyone who lies is committing a grave sin. Your tongue can encourage and comfort others or hurt and degrade others. Always speak with gentleness and kindness. Do not gossip nor put others to shame. Think before you speak. Be ready to listen more and slow to speak. Guard your tongue and speak only the truth."

Thank you, Jesus, for showing me the gravity of sin in lying. Help me always to speak with love and truth.

REFLECTION: Do I gossip and put people down instead of speaking words of encouragement and the truth?

DEAD ARE RAISED

"The blind regain their sight, the lame walk, lepers
are cleansed, the deaf hear, the dead are raised,
the poor have the good news proclaimed to them."

LUKE 7:22

In my vision Jesus was holding a little girl's hand and said, "Rise up!" and the dead child sat up from her bed. "My beloved, do you believe that I am the resurrection and the life? Whoever believes in me will have abundant life. For I am not a God of the dead but of the living. I come to heal and restore life. I come to set the captives free and to proclaim the good news to everyone. And yet people hate me and want to persecute me. Do not be afraid. Go and lay hands on the sick and pray for their healing. Proclaim the good news to those who need to hear it. Be my mouth and my hands to my people."

Yes, Lord Jesus, I will go and pray
with the sick and to tell them the good
news. Use me for I am yours.

REFLECTION: Do I truly believe that Jesus is the resurrection and the life?

FULLNESS OF PEACE

> *"Justice shall flourish in his time,*
> *and fullness of peace forever."*
> PSALM 72:7

In my vision I saw a river flowing between two banks with green trees and beautiful flowers all around it. "My precious one, peace be with you. My peace I give to you. Just like in your vision when you have peace in your heart you will reap goodness and joy everywhere you go. I will bring hope to those who are hopeless. My peace will flow out from you to everyone who feels troubled and burdened with worry. Tell my people that I am coming soon. I am the Prince of Peace and I bring great tidings to everyone who feels lonely and forgotten."

> *O my Jesus, thank you for giving us your*
> *peace and joy during this holy season. Fill*
> *our hearts with gratitude and hope.*

REFLECTION: Do I tell others that Jesus is the Prince of Peace and that he came to bring us hope?

EMMANUEL

> *"Behold the virgin shall be with child*
> *and bear a son, and they shall name him*
> *Emmanuel, which means 'God is with us.'"*
>
> MATTHEW 1:23

In my vision I saw myself as a child holding Jesus' right hand and on his left he was holding many other children. "My child, I will never leave you nor forsake you. You are the apple of my eye. You are always with me. You can count on me. Hold on to me and you will be safe. Do not let go of my hand. I will protect and shield you from the evil one. You need not worry. Like my mother Mary, live each day in my presence. Hold me tight and bring me everywhere you go. I will guide you and guard you from all harm. Rest assured that I will be with you till the end of time."

Most precious Jesus, I know you are always with
me. Let me never be separated away from you.

REFLECTION: Do I live each day in the presence of God and bring Him everywhere I go?

GOOD NEWS

"I am Gabriel, who stand before God.
I was sent to speak to you and to
announce to you this good news."

LUKE 1:19

In my vision I saw a beautiful angel with wings all aglow with light bringing good news to Mary. "Rejoice, my precious one, I am coming soon to bring blessings to you and your family. For you have found favor with God. I come so that all your sins are wiped away. You have been redeemed and restored to be God's beloved child and His eyes are always upon you. I will fill your heart with peace, love and joy. I will wipe away all your tears. Rejoice and be glad. My angels and saints are singing that I have come into the world to save you. Sing praise and thanksgiving all day long."

Lord Jesus, I praise you and thank
you for coming into the world to save
me. My heart overflows with joy.

REFLECTION: Is my heart filled with love, peace and joy just knowing that Jesus will soon be here with us?

HANDMAID

*"Behold, I am the handmaid of the Lord. May
it be done to me according to your word."*

LUKE 1:38

In my vision I saw a woman mopping a floor on her
hands and knees. "My child, Mary my mother did
everything for me. No job was too lowly for her. She was
the most obedient person in the world. As soon as she
heard that her elderly cousin Elizabeth was with child,
she went in haste to help her. She was always thinking
of other people's needs before her own. My mother was
willing to sacrifice herself and lay down her life for me.
She never called attention to herself but was always
inviting everyone to come to me instead. She was my
most faithful disciple. Imitate her and you will be holy."

*My Jesus, I do desire to be your handmaid and
your servant like your mother Mary. Help
me to be more obedient as she was to you.*

REFLECTION: Am I willing to sacrifice myself and be
a disciple of Jesus like Mary did?

YOU WHO BELIEVED

"Blessed are you who believed that what was spoken to you by the Lord would be fulfilled."

Luke 1:45

In my vision I saw a woman trying to touch Jesus' hem and she was instantly healed. "My little one, many people pray for things and healings but in their hearts they do not believe that I will give them what they asked for. They lack faith and trust in me. When the angel told Mary that she was to conceive a son, she believed that even though she was a virgin. Do you believe that nothing is impossible for me? If your answer is 'yes' then you will see miracles happening all the time. You will be able to do great things for me when you have faith in me."

Jesus, son of the living God, I do believe. Help my unbelief. With you all things are possible.

REFLECTION: Do I have faith in Jesus and trust him with all my heart?

GOOD THINGS

*"He has filled the hungry with good things
and the rich he has sent away empty."*

LUKE 1:53

In my vision I saw a table full of good food ready to be consumed. "My loving child, come to my banquet that I have prepared for you. Those who are hungry will be filled with my blessings. Those who are self-sufficient will go away empty. Come to me with open arms like a little child on Christmas day. I will lavish you with good gifts and graces upon you and your family. You will be filled with my peace, love and joy. Come hungry for my word and you will be satisfied. Make room in your heart and mind for me and you will be transformed and your life will never be the same again."

*Come, Lord Jesus, come into my heart
and soul. I am hungry for your love
and your words of wisdom.*

REFLECTION: Have I made room to welcome Jesus in my heart during this holy season?

YOUR REDEMPTION

"Lift up your heads and see, your redemption is near at hand."

LUKE 21:28

In my vision I saw Jesus descending from heaven with radiant light. "My precious child, yes, I am your redeemer and savior. Prepare your heart to receive me. Look up and you will see me coming. Many people are so busy with their daily lives that they never take time out to seek me. They are only concerned with their chores here on earth. Little do they realize that their time spent here is very short compared with eternal life with me in heaven. When you are focused on me everything you do will have true meaning. Store treasures in heaven. Seek me first and everything will be given to you."

Lord Jesus, my heart yearns to be united with you one day. Thank you for being my savior and my redeemer.

REFLECTION: Do I take time out of my busy life to seek Jesus who is coming soon?

MIGHTY SAVIOR

"Blessed be the Lord, the God of Isaiah; for
he has come to his people and set them free.
He has raised up for us a might Savior."
LUKE 1:68-69

In my vision I saw Jesus on the cross with blood stream-ing down his face. "My faithful one, I came into the world to show you what real love is like. It is not by hatred or violence that you can conquer evil around you, but through sacrificial love. There is no greater love than one who lays down one's life for another. Through my cross I have shown you the way, the truth and the life. Live each day by sacrificing yourself for those who need you most. Be my love to them. Let your light and joy shine everywhere you go during this Christmas Season."

Thank you, Jesus, for being my mighty Savior.
Fill me with more of your love so that I will
truly reflect your light and love to others.

REFLECTION: Do I live each day by sacrificing myself for the love of others as Jesus did for me?

JESUS WAS BORN

"Jesus was born in Bethlehem of Judea,
in the days of King Herod."

MATTHEW 2:1

In my vision I saw Mary holding baby Jesus lovingly in her arms in the manger. "My little one, I came as a baby so everyone can come close to me and not be frightened. I was placed in a manger to be food for your journey. Without me you will perish. With me you will be filled with the Holy Spirit and he will guide you and lead you to my Father's house. Hold me tight like my mother Mary. Always remember that I live within you. I am your bread of life. With me you will have abundant life. I came into the world so that you will be saved from all your sins."

Loving Jesus, you are my hope and my
savior. Without you I will perish. Thank
you for coming into this world to save us.

REFLECTION: Have I invited Jesus into my heart and held him tight in my arms as Mary did?

BE GLAD

*"Be glad in the Lord, you just, and
give thanks to his holy name."*
PSALM 97:12

In my vision I saw the shepherds' faces filled with joy
when they found Jesus in the manger. "My beloved, you
can always find me in the church waiting for you every
day. Have no anxiety whatsoever and live each day with
me in your heart and soul. Only in this way you will be
filled with peace and gratitude. Give thanks for all that I
have done for you. You are my treasure and I will always
love you with all my heart. You are more precious to me
than gold and silver. You belong to me. Be glad and sing
a joyful song and know that I am with you forever."

*I praise you and I adore you, my precious
Jesus. My soul sings with joy knowing that I
belong to you and you are always with me.*

REFLECTION: Do I sing praises to Jesus for all that
he has done for me?

THE CHILD

> *"Rise, take the child and his mother, flee to*
> *Egypt, and stay there until I tell you."*
>
> MATTHEW 2:13

In my vision I saw Jesus when he was a child dressed in a richly embroidered robe with a gold crown on his head. "My precious one, every child is created in my image and likeness. Treat each child with love and respect for they are very special to me. I cherish every one of them. Each child is unique and a gift from God. So many people do not realize this truth. They abuse their children instead of loving and teaching them. Many babies are aborted before they were born. There is no future without children in this world. They are your treasure. Love them as I love you."

> *Lord Jesus, give me more love for the children*
> *especially those who are handicapped.*
> *Protect them from all harm.*

REFLECTION: Do I treat each child with compassionate love and respect?

GOD IS LIGHT

*"God is light, and in him there
is no darkness at all."*

1 JOHN 1:5

In my vision I saw Jesus standing with Moses and Elijah and his clothes became dazzling white. "My child, when you are with me, you too will be in the light. You will see everything more clearly. You will understand the truth. So come to me often and let my light shine upon you. My light will guide you wherever you need to go. For I am the light of the world. With me you will be able to see the world with my eyes. You will not be in darkness. You will have clarity and confidence to walk on the right path. Live each day in my light and you will be saved."

*My sweet Jesus, you are my light and my
salvation. I will follow you wherever you go.
Let me never be separated away from you.*

REFLECTION: Do I see the world with the light of Christ?

PUT ON LOVE

"Over all these put on love, that
is the bound of perfection."
COLOSSIANS 3:14

In my vision I saw Joseph putting on his colorful coat which his father made especially for him. "My beloved, when you have love, you have everything you need. Everyone needs love. So put on love, not any love but MY love. When you experience my love for you then you will be able to love others. Love can move mountains. Love can change a heart of stone into a heart of flesh. Love gives hope and joy to others. Love endures forever. So live each day with my love in your heart and you will be able to change this world into a better place for everyone."

Loving Jesus, fill me with more of your love so that
I will be able to love others as you have loved me.

REFLECTION: Do I love everyone with the love of Christ in my heart?

UNION WITH HIM

*"This is the way we may know that we are
in union with him: whoever claims to abide
in him ought to walk just as he walked."*

1 JOHN 2:5-6

In my vision I saw myself walking with Jesus laughing and enjoying our journey together. "My faithful one, when you put me first in your life, you are walking with me. Make every decision based on what I want you to do. This is what happens when you are in union with me. You will try your best to do what pleases me, which will also benefit yourself, because my way is always the best way for you. I do everything with you in mind. I come to give you an abundant life, a life full of joy and hope. So do not wander off on your own but walk in unison with me."

*Jesus, you know the way to true happiness.
I want to follow you always and walk
with you till the end of my life.*

REFLECTION: Do I walk in unison with Jesus every day of my life?

GLORY

*"And the Word became flesh and make
his dwelling among us, and we saw
his glory, the glory as the Father's only
begotten son, full of grace and truth."*

JOHN 1:14

In my vision I saw resurrected Jesus sitting on the right hand of his Father with glorious radiance. "My precious child, one day you too will be in heaven united with me and my Father. You will receive your crown for all you have done for my glory. You will be honored and loved by all. For you have been a faithful servant. Your heart is pure and you did what is pleasing in my sight. Come, my love, come and share my joy. Never give up striving to be closer to me. For I will bless everything you do for my honor and glory. Tomorrow is a New Year and a new beginning for you. Go in peace."

*Lord Jesus, Son of the living God, may
you be honored and glorified forever.
I praise you and I adore you!*

REFLECTION: Are all my actions pure and pleasing to Jesus so that they will glorify him in everything I do?

ADDENDA

About St. John Eudes

Born in France on November 14, 1601, St. John Eudes' life spanned the "Great Century." The Age of Discovery had revolutionized technology and exploration; the Council of Trent initiated a much-needed reform in the Church; among the common people, it was the dawn of a golden age of sanctity and mystic fervor.

HIS SPIRITUAL HERITAGE

No fewer than seven Doctors of the Church had lived in the previous century. Great reformers like St. Francis de Sales, St. Teresa of Avila, and St. John of the Cross had left an indelible mark on the Catholic faith. Their influence was still fresh as St. John Eudes came onto the scene.

He was educated by the Jesuits in rural Normandy. He was ordained into the Oratory of Jesus and Mary, a society of priests which had just been founded on the model of St. Philip Neri's Oratory in Rome. The founder was Cardinal Pierre de Bérulle, a man renowned for his holiness and named "the apostle of the Incarnate Word" by Pope Urban VII. Rounding out St. John Eudes' heritage is the influence of the Discalced Carmelites. His spiritual director, Cardinal Bérulle himself, had brought sisters from St. Teresa of Avila's convent to help found the Carmel in France. John Eudes would later become spiritual director to a Carmelite convent himself. Their cloister prayed constantly for his missionary activity.

HIS LIFE OF MINISTRY

As an avid participant in a wave of re-evangelization in France, St. John Eudes' principal apostolate was preaching parish missions. Spending anywhere from 4 to 20 weeks in each parish, he preached over 120 missions across his lifetime, always with a team of confessors providing the sacrament around the clock, and catechists meeting daily with small groups of parishioners.

Early in his priesthood, an outbreak of plague hit St. John Eudes' native region and he rushed to provide sacraments to the dying. The risk of contagion was so great no one else dared to approach the victims. In order to protect his Oratorian brothers from contagion, St. John Eudes took up residence in a large empty cider barrel outside of the city walls until the plague had ended.

HIS FOUNDATIONS

During his missions, he heard countless confessions himself, including those from women forced into prostitution. Realizing that they needed intense healing and support, he began to found "Houses of Refuge" to help them get off the street and begin a new life. In 1641 he founded the Sisters of Our Lady of Charity of the Refuge to continue this work. They would live with the penitent women and provide them with constant support. Today, these sisters are known as the Good Shepherd Sisters, inspired by their fourth vow of zeal to go out seeking the "lost sheep."

Occasionally, St. John Eudes would return to the site of a previous mission. To his dismay, he found that the fruits of the mission were consistently fading for lack of support. The crucial piece in need of change was the priesthood. At that time, the only way to be trained as a priest was through apprenticeship. The result of this training was so horribly inconsistent that the term "hocus pocus" was invented during this time to describe the corrupted Latin used by poorly trained priests during the consecration at mass. In 1643 he left the Oratory and founded the Congregation of Jesus and Mary to create a seminary. Seminary training was a radical brand-new concept which had just been proposed by the Council of Trent.

HIS MARK ON THE CHURCH

At a mission in 1648 St. John Eudes authored the first mass in history in honor of the Heart of Mary. In 1652 he built the first church under the Immaculate Heart's patronage: the chapel of his seminary in Coutances, France. During the process of his canonization, Pope St. Pius X named St. John Eudes "the father, doctor, and apostle of liturgical devotion to the hearts of Jesus and Mary." The Heart of Jesus because he created the first Feast of the Sacred Heart in 1672, just one year before St. Margaret Mary Alacoque had her first apparition of the Sacred Heart.

Although his Marian devotion was intense from a tender age, the primary inspiration for this feast came from St. John Eudes' theology of baptism. From the beginning of his missionary career, he taught that Jesus continues His Incarnation in the life of each baptized Christian. As we give ourselves to Christ, our hands become His hands, our heart is transformed into His heart. Mary is the ultimate exemplar of this. She gave her heart to God so completely that she and Jesus have just one heart between them. Thus, whoever sees Mary, sees Jesus, and honoring the heart of Mary is never separate from honoring the heart of Jesus.

DOCTOR OF THE CHURCH?

At the time of this writing, Bishops the world over have requested that the Vatican proclaim St. John Eudes as a Doctor of the Church. This would recognize his unique contribution to our understanding of the Gospel, and his exemplary holiness of life which stands out even among saints. For more information on the progress of this cause, on his writings or spirituality, or to sign up for our e-newsletter updates, contact spirituality@eudistsusa.org.

About the Eudist Family

During his lifetime, St. John Eudes' missionary activity had three major areas of focus.

+ For priests, he provided formation, education, and the spiritual support which is crucial for their role in God's plan of salvation.

+ For prostitutes and others on the margins of society, he gave them a home and bound their wounds, like the Good Shepherd with his lost sheep.

+ For the laity, he preached the dignity of their baptism and their responsibility to be the hands and feet of God, to continue the Incarnation.

In everything he did, he burned with the desire to be a living example of the love and mercy of God.

These are the "family values" which continue to inspire those who continue his work. To paraphrase St. Paul, John Eudes planted seeds, which others watered through the institutions he founded, and God gave the growth. Today, the family tree continues to bear fruit:

The *Congregation of Jesus and Mary* (CJM), also known as The Eudists, continues the effort to form and care for priests and other leaders within the Church. St. John Eudes called this the mission of "teaching the teachers, shepherding the shepherds, and enlightening those who are the light of the world." Continuing his efforts as a missionary preacher, Eudist priests and brothers "audaciously seek to open up new avenues for evangelization," through television, radio, and new media.

The *Religious of the Good Shepherd* (RGS) continue outreach to women in difficult situations, providing them with a deeply needed place of refuge and healing while they seek a new life. St. Mary Euphrasia drastically expanded the reach of this mission which now operates in over 70 countries worldwide. A true heiress of St. John Eudes, St. Mary Euphrasia exhorted her sisters: "We must go after the lost sheep with no other rest than the cross, no other consolation than work, and no other thirst than for justice."

In every seminary and House of Refuge founded by St. John Eudes, he also established a *Confraternity of the Holy Heart of Jesus and Mary* for the laity, now known as the Eudist Associates. The mission he gave them was twofold: First, "To glorify the divine Hearts of Jesus and Mary... working to make them live and reign in their own heart through diligent imitation of their virtues." Second, "To work for the salvation of souls... by practicing, according to their abilities, works of charity and mercy and by attaining numerous graces through prayer for the clergy and other apostolic laborers."

The *Little Sisters of the Poor* were an outgrowth of this confraternity. St. Jeanne Jugan was formed as a consecrated woman within the Eudist Family. She discovered the great need for love and mercy among the poor and elderly and the mission took on a life of its own. She passed on to them the Eudist intuition that the poor are not simply recipients of charity, they provide an encounter with Charity Himself: "My little ones, never forget that the poor are Our Lord... In serving the aged, it is He Himself whom you are serving."

A more recent "sprout" on the tree was founded by Mother Antonia Brenner in Tijuana, Mexico. After raising her children in Beverly Hills and suffering through divorce, she followed God's call to become a live-in prison minister at the *La Mesa* penitentiary. The *Eudist Servants of the 11th Hour* was founded so that other women in the latter part of their lives could imitate her in "being love" to those most in need.

The example St. John Eudes set for living out the Gospel has inspired many more individuals and organizations throughout the world. For more information about the Eudist family, news on upcoming publications, or for ways to share in our mission, contact us at spirituality@eudistsusa.org.

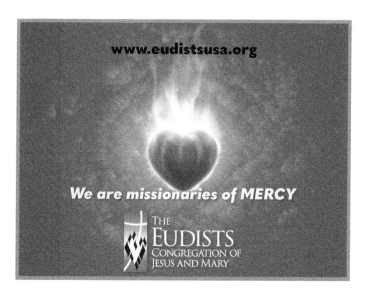

More by Eudist Press

+ *A Heart on Fire: St. John Eudes, a Model*
  for the New Evangelization
+ *Spiritual Itinerary for Today with St. John Eudes*
+ *Eudist Lectionary: A St. John Eudes Reader*

Eudist Prayerbook Series
+ Volume 1: *Heart of the Holy Family:*
  A Manual of Prayer
+ Volume 2: *More than Just 50 Beads:*
  Rosary Meditations for the Liturgical Year
+ Volume 3: *A Holy Week Every Week:*
  Weekday Meditations
+ Volume 4: *34 Flames of Divine Love:*
  Elevations of the Heart Towards God
+ Volume 5: *On the Threshold of Life:*
  A Self-Directed Retreat to Celebrate your Birthday
+ Volume 6: *On the Threshold of Eternity:*
  A Self-Directed Retreat to Prepare for a Happy Death

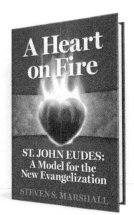

Biography
+ *St. John Eudes: Worker for the*
  New Evangelization in the 17th Century
+ *In All Things, the Will of God:*
  St. John Eudes Through His Letters

More by St. John Eudes

St. John Eudes' Selected Works

+ *The Life and Kingdom of Jesus in Christian Souls*
+ *The Sacred Heart of Jesus*
+ *The Admirable Heart of Mary*
+ *The Priest: His Dignity and Obligations*
+ *Meditations*
+ *Letters and Shorter Works*

Other Works

+ *Man's Contract with God in Holy Baptism*
+ *The Wondrous Childhood of the Mother of God*

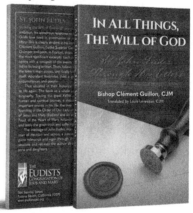

Visit the
Eudist Bookstore
at
www.bit.ly/SJEudes

About the author

Lily L. Loh is the author of several books. She studied in St. Mary's College and has a B.S. from Purdue University and majored in Home Economics. Her M.A. degree is from Cornell University where she also taught for two years. She was a fashion designer in New York City. When she and her husband moved to San Diego, Lily owned a Cooking School and taught classes for twenty one years. She was invited to do cooking demonstrations on several TV shows, including CNN. After her retirement she taught religious classes and was a Healing Prayer Minister and Eucharistic Minister at St. James Church in Solana Beach, California. Lily is a widow and a mother of two children and four grandsons. She has travelled around the world and lived in four different continents.

Lily can be contacted at
ListenToGodDaily@yahoo.com

Made in the USA
Middletown, DE
29 December 2022

17854832R00230